RAPTURE FUSION

Merging the Pre-Tribulation,
Mid-Tribulation, Pre-Wrath, and
Post-Tribulation Rapture Views into
Something Better

Brent D. Humason

Dedication

I am dedicated to my wonderful wife, Elisabeth Humason, as is this book. I am so thankful she still loves me, even though I put a dragon (Revelation 12:4) in our kids' nativity scene.

> 4 And his tail swept away a third of the stars of heaven and threw them to the earth. And the dragon stood before the woman who was about to give birth, so that when she gave birth he might devour her child. (Revelation 12:4)

A big thank you to Katheryn Feather and Elisabeth Humason for the heroic editing. It was not easy turning a software engineer into an author.

I would also like to give special thanks to Arthur Anderson and Jeff Bohlin who each provided excellent feedback on draft versions of this book. My life group also deserves thanks for giving me the idea to write a book about what I learned while teaching on Revelation. I am grateful for all of the pastors and Bible teachers who have led me over the years, especially Pastor Josh Matlock who started me on this end times journey.

Above all, I would like to thank God for answering so many of my prayers in bringing this book together.

Table of Contents

Part I: Introduction..1
   Introduction to Rapture Fusion....................................3
   Introduction to Revelation..7
   Introduction to the Millennium..................................13
   Introduction Summary..19
Part II: Four Pre-Millennial Views..23
   Pre-Tribulation Pre-Millennial View..........................25
   Mid-Tribulation Pre-Millennial View.........................41
   Pre-Wrath Pre-Millennial View...................................51
   Post-Tribulation Pre-Millennial View.........................61
Part III: Rapture Fusion...69
   What is Rapture Fusion?..71
   What is Recapitulation?...75
   Where is Recapitulation in Revelation?.......................81
   How is Recapitulation used in Rapture Fusion?.........133
Part IV: Reexamining the Pre-Millennial Rapture Views.........149
   Reexamining the Post-Tribulation Rapture................151
   Reexamining the Pre-Wrath Rapture.........................155
   Reexamining the Mid-Tribulation Rapture................167
   Reexamining the Pre-Tribulation Rapture.................173
Part V: Conclusion..189
   Rapture Prerequisites..191
   Summary..203
Glossary..207
Bible Reference Index..221
About the Author...235

Part I:
Introduction

Introduction to Rapture Fusion

My main prayer for this book is that it will help keep readers from being deceived. Three times in our Lord's sermon on His return, He warned us not to be misled. The sermon is known as the "Olivet Discourse," and is found in Matthew 24, Mark 13 and Luke 21. [1]

> 4 And Jesus answered and said to them, "<u>See to it that no one misleads you</u>. (Matthew 24:4)
>
> 10 "At that time <u>many will fall away</u> and will betray one another and hate one another.
> 11 "Many false prophets will arise and <u>will mislead many</u>. (Matthew 24:10-11)

---

[1] Throughout this book I will quote from the New American Standard Bible (NASB) unless otherwise noted. The italics, in the NASB, indicate that the word was not in the original language, but was added to make more sense in English. I added the underscores, to point out why I am including the passage. I will also direct the reader to a glossary at the back of the book.

24 "For false Christs and false prophets will arise and will show great signs and wonders, <u>so as to mislead, if possible, even the elect</u>. (Matthew 24:24)

In the context of the coming of our Lord Jesus Christ, Paul also warned us not to be deceived.

1 Now we request you, brethren, with regard to the <u>coming of our Lord Jesus Christ</u> and <u>our gathering</u> together to Him,
2 that you not be quickly shaken from your composure or be disturbed either by a spirit or a message or a letter as if from us, to the effect that <u>the day of the Lord</u> has come.
3 <u>Let no one in any way deceive you</u>, for *it will not come* unless the <u>apostasy comes first</u>, and the man of lawlessness is revealed, the son of destruction, (2 Thessalonians 2:1-3)

Most, if not all, godly men and women are deceived in some way about the end times. Just statistically speaking, there are so many end time views: Preterists, Historicists, Idealists, and Futurists. Then combine those with A-Millennialists, Post-Millennialists, and Pre-Millennialists, and subdivide those with Pre-Tribulationalists, Mid-Tribulationalists, Pre-Wrath, and Post-Tribulationalists. Even if any one of those views is completely right, then most of Christendom is wrong, and was deceived. Chances are, I am deceived, at least in part, as well. I know a lot more about the end times now than I did ten years ago, and I pray, ten years from now I will know more than I do today. As A.T. Pierson wrote about how my hero, George Müller, changed his position on baptism, he said, "Don't be consistent, but simply be true!" (George Müller of Bristol, Location 772). We need to remain teachable. Being teachable is a part of humility. Once we stop being teachable, pride has set in.

With this in mind, please test everything I have written with the scriptures. The apostle Paul commended the Bereans for doing so, and how much more so, should you test what I write with the scriptures.

> 11 Now these were more noble-minded than those in Thessalonica, for they received the word with great eagerness, examining the Scriptures daily to see whether these things were so. (Acts 17:11)

There are three ways in which I hope this book keeps you from being deceived. First, that the book would help you know when the rapture will take place relative to other end times events. Second, that it helps you understand the structure of Revelation so you can read and understand it clearly. Finally, but most importantly, if you do not have a right relationship with Jesus Christ, that you would change that today. In Revelation, Jesus said to the Church at Laodicea,

> 16 So then, because you are lukewarm, and neither cold nor hot, I will vomit you out of My mouth. (Revelation 3:16 NKJV)

There were two towns near Laodicea, with two sources of water, one was cold and good for drinking, the other was hot and good for bathing. By the time the two waters came to Laodicea they were lukewarm, and good for nothing. Therefore, it can be inferred from the passage that both the hot and the cold are believing churches and are useful, but the lukewarm is the unbelieving church which will be spit out. Jesus said of those who are lukewarm, that He would "vomit you out of My mouth" (NKJV), and are "wretched and miserable and poor and blind and naked" (Revelation 3:17). If you are a lukewarm church attendee, you should fear being vomited out of Jesus' mouth. Francis Chan put it this way,

> As I see it, a lukewarm Christian is an Oxymoron; there is no such thing. To put it plainly, churchgoers who are "lukewarm" are not Christians. We will not see them in heaven. (Francis Chan, *Crazy Love*, pg 83-84)

As you read of the Revelation of Jesus Christ, I pray He will reveal Himself to you, and that you would let Him into your life. Just a few verses later it is written:

> 20 'Behold, I stand at the door and knock; <u>if anyone hears My voice and opens the door</u>, I will come in to him and will dine with him, and he with Me. (Revelation 3:20)

I do not want you to be deceived about the rapture, Revelation, nor your relationship to the coming King.

Introduction to Revelation

There are four basic ways to read Revelation:

Preterist – Everything (Full Preterist) or nearly everything (Partial Preterist) in Revelation has been fulfilled.

Historicist – Everything in Revelation is continually being fulfilled from the first century until now.

Idealist – Revelation is like a parable about the battle between good and evil.

Futurist – Nearly everything in Revelation will take place in the future.

Preterist

Preterists believe everything (Full Preterists) or nearly everything (Partial Preterists) in Revelation was fulfilled by 70 AD. For this view, they require Revelation to be written before 70 AD. The main problem with the Preterist view is that Jesus did not return and gather the elect in 70 AD.

30 "And then the sign of the Son of Man will appear in the sky, and then all the tribes of the earth will mourn, and they will see the Son of Man coming on the clouds of the sky with power and great glory.
31 "And He will send forth His angels with a great trumpet and they will gather together His elect from the four winds, from one end of the sky to the other. (Matthew 24:30-31)

Jesus said all the prophesies in Matthew 24 needed to be fulfilled in the same generation.

34 "Truly I say to you, this generation will not pass away until all these things take place. (Matthew 24:34)

The generation that sees all the events in Matthew 24, like the "abomination of desolation," will not pass away until they see Jesus coming and the elect gathered. Since the gathering did not take place in that first century generation, it all needs to be fulfilled in a future generation.

Historicist

Historicists view things like the beast from the sea (Revelation 13:1-10), and the beast from the earth (Revelation 13:11-18), as having been attacking the Christians from the first century until today. They would not say the beast is a single person or entity, but represents a constant threat to the church throughout the ages. Some Historicists say the Pope is the beast, since there is always a Pope, that way all of Revelation is always applicable. The main point of Historicists, is they want it to be applicable to every generation. While Revelation is applicable to every generation, for example we all need to be reminded to worship God (Revelation 22:9), are blessed by reading Revelation (Revelation 1:3), and look forward to the coming King (Revelation 19:11-16). Revelation is not being fulfilled repeatedly in every generation. This view throws out all the specific references to time in Revelation. Forty-two months (Revelation 11:2) would not be a fixed period of time, but last the entire church age, and would be no different than the 5 months (Revelation 9:10) of locust (demon) attacks, which Historicists would also say spans the entire church age. Daniel is one of the books most similar to Revelation, and its symbols were fulfilled by specific people, at specific periods of time, after Daniel's life. For example, the prophesy of Alexander the Great and his kingdom being split up into four (Daniel 8:5-8, 21-22) was prophesied as a horn and four horns that took its place. Furthermore, the prophesied periods of time in Daniel were fulfilled to the day,

> 25 Now listen and understand! Seven sets of seven plus sixty-two sets of seven will pass from the time the command is given to rebuild Jerusalem until a ruler—the Anointed One—comes. Jerusalem will be rebuilt with streets and strong defenses, despite the perilous times. (Daniel 9:25 NLT)

The seven sets of seven years (49 years) plus 62 sets of seven years (434 years) are a total of 483 years. The 483 years start from the issuing of a decree to rebuild Jerusalem, and end with Messiah the prince. Nehemiah 2 provides the date that the "command is given to rebuild Jerusalem." From that date (Nisan, in the twentieth year of King Artaxerxes), by adding 483 (360 day) years, we are brought to the triumphal entry of Jesus at the start of Holy Week, exactly 483 years from when the command to rebuild Jerusalem was given, and fulfilled Daniel 9:25. We can trust the specific times in the prophesies. We should not just ignore numbers like 42 months and 5 months, and call them both the church age. The prophecies in Revelation are yet to be fulfilled.

Idealist

The Idealist view treats Revelation as a parable. Idealists say it is just meant to show Jesus triumphs over evil, but they do not think we should take Revelation any further than that. The passages in the Bible that are well-known as parables are analogies, each with a single spiritual purpose to convey. Parables are not meant to be dissected to find multiple meanings. Idealists believe we should treat Revelation the same way. This view fails similarly to the Historicist view. Daniel's prophesies were not parables, but were actually fulfilled (or are yet to be fulfilled). Since both Daniel and Revelation are apocalyptic books, we know the events in Revelation will actually be fulfilled. Apocalyptic books are a genre of books in the Bible that unveil the future.

Futurist

The Futurist view holds that most of Revelation is in the future. John and Jesus provide an outline for the book:

> "Therefore write the things which you have seen, and the things which are, and the things which will take place after these things. (Revelation 1:19)

Revelation 1 contains "the things which you [John] have seen." John had just seen the vision of Jesus, the stars, and the lampstands. Revelation 2-3 are the seven letters to the first-century churches, current to John's day and "the things which are." Chapters 4-22 describe "the things which will take place after these things" (Revelation 1:19). While Revelation is full of symbols, the events that are symbolized have been or will be fulfilled in the future, and the measures of time can be taken literally. We can assume 5 months means 5 months and 42 months means 42 months or, at a minimum, that 42 months is longer than 5 months. Rapture Fusion will utilize the Futurist method of reading Revelation.

Introduction to the Millennium

By definition, a millennium is 1,000 years. While the word "millennium" is not used in the Bible, "1,000 years" is mentioned six times in Revelation 20. It is joked to be the 1,000 years of peace that Christians like to fight about. The three main views revolve around the relationship between the return of Christ and the Millennial Kingdom. There are actually two millennial debates; whether the millennium is a literal or a figurative 1,000 years, and if the kingdom is a spiritual kingdom with Jesus ruling from Heaven through the Church, or if it will be a future physical kingdom with Jesus ruling on the earth with the Church. The three millennial views are:

A-Millennial – Jesus will return after a figurative 1,000 year spiritual kingdom.

Post-Millennial – Jesus will return after a literal 1,000 year spiritual kingdom, but it is unknown when the 1,000 years start.

Pre-Millennial – Jesus will return before a literal 1,000 year physical kingdom.

A-Millennial

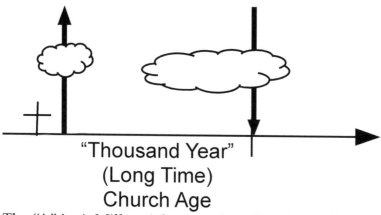

"Thousand Year" (Long Time) Church Age

The "A" in A-Millennial means "not," and A-Millennialists believe it is not a literal 1,000 years, rather a figurative millennium. Also, they believe Jesus will return after the figurative millennial spiritual kingdom. Some prefer the term "realized millennium" because it is being realized now, as opposed to not believing in a millennial kingdom. For this view, 1,000 years just means a long time, not exactly 1,000 years. Just as in, where God owns the cattle on a thousand hills does not mean God owns the cattle on exactly 1,000 hills, it means He owns the cattle on a large number of hills, or all of the hills.

> 10 "For every beast of the forest is Mine,
> The cattle on a <u>thousand hills</u>. (Psalm 50:10)

In a similar way, A-Millennialists say the millennial kingdom will last a very long time, not exactly 1,000 years. They believe the millennium is a spiritual kingdom, and the kingdom of God is in you.

> 21 nor will they say, 'Look, here *it is!*' or, 'There *it is!*' For behold, <u>the kingdom of God is in your midst</u>." (Luke 17:21)

Post-Millennial

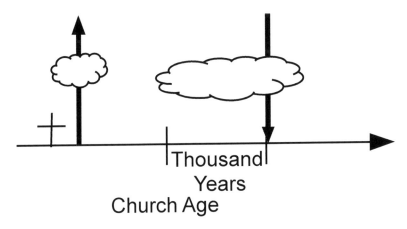

Thousand
Years
Church Age

"Post" means "after," so Post-Millennialists believe Jesus will return after a literal 1,000 year kingdom. However, it is unknown when the 1,000 years start. Post-Millennialism is similar to A-Millennialism in that they both believe in a spiritual kingdom, with the kingdom of God in believers. Post-Millennialism is also similar to Pre-Millennialism in that they both believe in a literal 1,000 years.

Pre-Millennial

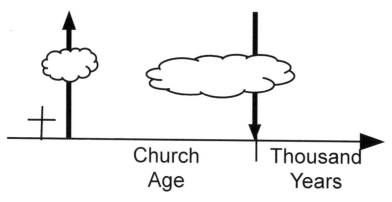

Church
Age

Thousand
Years

"Pre" means "before," so Pre-millinnialists believe Christ will return before a literal 1,000 year kingdom. Pre-millennialists believe there will be a physical kingdom on earth, just as we pray in the Lord's Prayer.

> 10 'Your <u>kingdom come</u>.
> Your will be done,
> <u>On earth</u> as it is in heaven. (Matthew 6:10)

The Millennial debate is primarily based on three different interpretations of one verse.

> 4 Then I saw thrones, and they sat on them, and judgment was given to them. And I *saw* the <u>souls</u> of those who had been beheaded because of their testimony of Jesus and because of the word of God, and those who had not worshiped the beast or his image, and had not received the mark on their forehead and on their hand; and <u>they came to life</u> and <u>reigned with Christ for a thousand years</u>. (Revelation 20:4)

Pre-Millennialists believe these souls that come to life signify the Resurrection, and that the resurrected reign on earth for a thousand years, fulfilling the promise of Revelation 5:10.

> 10 "You have made them *to be* a <u>kingdom</u> and priests to our God; and <u>they will reign upon the earth.</u>" (Revelation 5:10)

Introduction Summary

The Preterist, Historicist, Idealist, and Futurist views can be overlaid with each of the A-Millennial, Post-Millennial, and Pre-Millennial views. For example, you could have a Preterist A-Millennial, a Historicist A-Millennial, an Idealist A-Millennial, or a Futurist A-Millennial view. On the following page is a table showing how each of the interpretation styles, overlaid with each of the Millennial views, might read various chapters as having already passed, occurring in the present, or as a future event.

Revelation Interpretation with Millennial View

	Preterist/ Partial Preterist (fulfilled)	Historicist (being fulfilled throughout the church age)	Idealist (parable)	Futurist (yet to be fulfilled)
A-millennialist	Rev. 1-19 Past, Rev. 20 Present, Rev. 21-22 Future	Rev. 1-20 Present, Rev. 21-22 Future	Rev. 1-20 Present, Rev. 21-22 Future	Rev. 1-3 Past, Rev. 20 Present, Rev. 4-19, 21-22 Future
Post-millennialist	Rev. 1-19 Past, Rev. 20-22 Future	Rev. 1-19 Present, Rev. 20 Present/ Future, Rev. 21-22 Future	Rev. 1-19 Present, Rev. 20 Present/ Future, Rev. 21-22 Future	Rev. 1-3 Past, Rev. 20 Present/ Future, Rev. 4-19, 21-22 Future
Pre-millennialist	Rev. 1-19 Past, Rev. 20-22 Future	Rev. 1-19 Present, Rev. 20-22 Future	Rev. 1-19 Present, Rev. 20-22 Future	Rev. 1-3 Past, Rev. 4-22 Future

Rapture Fusion will focus on the Futurist Pre-Millennial view, because I believe, as many prominent theologians do, that most of Revelation has yet to be fulfilled and the most common rapture views are part of the Pre-Millennial view. The Futurist Pre-Millennial view can be broken up into four different views. The four main views revolve around the relationship between the Rapture/Resurrection and the 7 Year Tribulation (AKA Daniel's seventieth seven, or Daniel's seventieth week). The four Pre-Millennial views are:

Pre-Trib – Rapture before the Tribulation

Mid-Trib – Rapture 3.5 Years into the Tribulation

Pre-Wrath – Rapture at the Sixth Seal

Post-Trib – Rapture at the End of the Tribulation

The following chapters will aim to explain the four Pre-Millennial views and how they can come together in Rapture Fusion.

Part II:
Four Pre-Millennial Views

There are four main Futurist Pre-Millennial views. In other words, of those who see Revelation 4-22 as future events and believe Christ will come back to earth before His 1,000 year (millennial) reign, there are four main theories as to when the rapture and resurrection will take place.

Some say the word "rapture" is not in the Bible. But, that is similar to saying the word "Señor" is not in the Bible. "Señor" is not in my Bible, nor is it in the original Greek, but if you have a Spanish Bible "Señor" is in the Bible. It is a similar deal with the word "rapture." It is not in my Bible, nor is it in the original Greek, but if you have a Latin Bible you can find the word from which we get rapture. The Latin word *rapiemur* is translated in our English Bibles as "caught up." Here is an example:

> 16 For the Lord Himself will descend from heaven with a shout, with the voice of the archangel and with the trumpet of God, and the <u>dead in Christ will rise first</u>.
> 17 <u>Then</u> we who are <u>alive</u> and remain will be <u>caught up</u> together with them in the clouds to meet the Lord in the air, and so we shall always be with the Lord. (1 Thessalonians 4:16-17)

The phrase "caught up" in 1 Thessalonians 4:17 is the rapture. Only those who are alive are "raptured." When the dead rise, it is called the "resurrection." The resurrection occurs first, then the rapture. This dual resurrection and rapture event is often just referred to as the rapture.

The four Futurist Pre-Millennial views differ on the timing of the rapture relative to other events. In this part of the book, I give a general description of each rapture position, but the pros and cons of each view will be presented in subsequent chapters.

Pre-Tribulation Pre-Millennial View

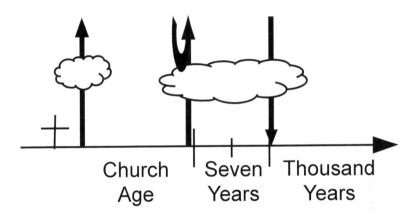

Church Age | Seven Years | Thousand Years

The Pre-Tribulation view places the rapture before seven years of tribulation, which will take place before the 1,000 year reign of Christ. The view holds that Jesus will descend from Heaven, to the clouds, believers will be caught up to Him, and He will return to Heaven with them. For the seven years after the rapture and resurrection there will be tribulation on earth. However, during the tribulation (after the believers have been caught up), more people come to Christ (tribulation saints) and start to live and die for Him. The fact that there are believers on earth between chapters 4-19 can be seen in several passages. One example of this can be seen in the answer to the martyrs' question at the 5th seal.

> 11 And there was given to each of them a white robe; and they were told that they should rest for a little while longer, until *the number of* their fellow servants and <u>their brethren</u> who were to be killed even as they had been, would be completed also. (Revelation 6:11)

So, after the seven years of tribulation, the Pre-Tribulation view requires a second rapture and a second resurrection for those who came to Christ during the tribulation. This follow-up rapture and resurrection is at the second coming of Jesus. From the Pre-Tribulation perspective, the second resurrection can be seen after Jesus comes to Earth, and the dead come to life, which is a resurrection.

> 4 Then I saw thrones, and they sat on them, and judgment was given to them. And I *saw* <u>the souls of those who had been beheaded</u> because of their testimony of Jesus and because of the word of God, and those who had not worshiped the beast or his image, and had not received the mark on their forehead and on their hand; and <u>they came to life</u> and reigned with Christ for a thousand years. (Revelation 20:4)

The second rapture, from the Pre-Tribulation perspective, can be seen after the seven year tribulation, when the believers are gathered "from one end of the sky to the other." Jesus was using a Hebrew phrase, "from one end of the heavens to the other" found in Deuteronomy 4:32. There is another Hebrew phrase, "from one end of the earth to the other end of the earth" found in Deuteronomy 28:64, Deuteronomy 13:7, and Jeremiah 25:33, that Jesus could have used. However, Jesus specifically chose the sky or heavens phrase instead of the earth phrase, because He is describing a gathering in the sky, a rapture. The gathering in the sky could only happen if the believers were "caught up," or raptured in the air in the first place.

> 29 "But <u>immediately after the tribulation</u> of those days THE SUN WILL BE DARKENED, AND THE MOON WILL NOT GIVE ITS LIGHT, AND THE STARS WILL FALL from the sky, and the powers of the heavens will be shaken.
>
> 30 "And then the sign of the Son of Man will appear in the sky, and then all the tribes of the earth will mourn, and they will see the SON OF MAN COMING ON THE CLOUDS OF THE SKY with power and great glory.
>
> 31 "And He will send forth His angels with A GREAT TRUMPET and THEY WILL <u>GATHER TOGETHER</u> His <u>elect from the four winds, from one end of the sky to the other</u>. (Matthew 24:29-31)

Those with the Pre-Tribulation view usually do not consider Jesus coming in the clouds before the tribulation to be the "second coming" because Jesus does not come all the way down to earth, as He does after the seven years. After the second coming at the end of the seven years of tribulation, the

1,000 year reign starts. At the end of the thousand-year reign is another resurrection, called the second death.

> 14 Then death and Hades were thrown into the lake of fire. This is <u>the second death, the lake of fire</u>.
> 15 And if <u>anyone's</u> name was <u>not</u> found written <u>in the book of life</u>, he was thrown into the <u>lake of fire</u>. (Revelation 20:14-15)

These are the order of events needed for the Pre-Tribulation view:

1. Resurrection (1 Thessalonians 4:16)

2. Rapture (1 Thessalonians 4:17)

3. Seven Years of Tribulation (Daniel 9:27)

4. Another Resurrection (Revelation 20:4)

5. Another Rapture (Matthew 24:29-31)

6. 2nd Coming (Hebrews 9:28)

7. 1,000 year reign (Revelation 20:4-6)

8. 2nd Death (Revelation 20:11-15)

To summarize what we have looked at so far, the Pre-Tribulation doctrine holds that there is a resurrection and rapture before seven years of tribulation. Now, let's take a closer look at where the concept of seven years of tribulation comes from. Daniel 9:24-27 can be a difficult passage to understand. For this passage, I like the interpenetrated translation (New Living Translation), as opposed to a word-for-word translation (NASB), because the NLT interprets it the way I, and many others, interpret it from the NASB. Keep in mind, one "set of seven" is seven years.

²⁴ "A period of <u>seventy sets of seven</u> has been decreed for your people and your holy city to finish their rebellion, to put an end to their sin, to atone for their guilt, to bring in everlasting righteousness, to confirm the prophetic vision, and to anoint the Most Holy Place.
²⁵ Now listen and understand! <u>Seven sets of seven plus sixty-two sets of seven</u> will pass from the time the command is given to <u>rebuild Jerusalem</u> until a ruler—<u>the Anointed One</u>—comes. Jerusalem will be rebuilt with streets and strong defenses, despite the perilous times.
²⁶ "<u>After this period of sixty-two sets of seven</u>, the Anointed One will be killed, appearing to have accomplished nothing, and a ruler will arise whose armies will destroy the city and the Temple. The end will come with a flood, and war and its miseries are decreed from that time to the very end.
²⁷ <u>The ruler</u> will make a treaty with the people for a period of <u>one set of seven</u>, but <u>after half this time</u>, <u>he will put an end to the sacrifices</u> and offerings. And as a climax to all his terrible deeds, <u>he will set up a sacrilegious object that causes desecration</u>, until the fate decreed for this defiler is finally poured out on him." (Daniel 9:24-27 NLT)

Gabriel told Daniel what was going to happen in the future. Each set of seven is seven years. So "seventy sets of seven" is seventy times seven years, which equals 490 years. Gabriel is giving Daniel a 490 year prophesy. Four-hundred ninety years is significant in this context. The chapter begins with a beautiful prayer from Daniel. He said the reason for his prayer was due to a 70-year prophesy from Jeremiah.

> 2 in the first year of his reign, I, Daniel, observed in the books the number of the years which was *revealed as* the word of the LORD to Jeremiah the prophet for the completion of the <u>desolations of Jerusalem</u>, *namely,* <u>seventy years</u>. (Daniel 9:2)

At this point, Daniel had spent about 70 years in exile, and was reminding God of the 70 year prophesy. But there is more to the 70 years. The reason Judea, and Daniel, were exiled for 70 years was to let the land of Israel rest for seventy years.

> 20 Those who had escaped from the sword he carried away to Babylon; and they were servants to him and to his sons until the rule of the kingdom of Persia,
> 21 to fulfill the word of the LORD by the mouth of Jeremiah, <u>until the land had enjoyed its sabbaths</u>. All the days of its desolation it kept sabbath until <u>seventy years</u> were complete. (2 Chronicles 36:20-21)

The land needed to rest for 70 years because God's law was not kept for 490 years. Israel was supposed to give the land a sabbatical rest every seven years.

> 1 The LORD then spoke to Moses at Mount Sinai, saying,
> 2 "Speak to the sons of Israel and say to them, 'When you come into the land which I shall give you, then <u>the land shall have a sabbath</u> to the LORD.

3 'Six years you shall sow your field, and six years you shall prune your vineyard and gather in its crop,
4 but <u>during the seventh year the land shall have a sabbath rest</u>, a sabbath to the LORD; you shall not sow your field nor prune your vineyard.
5 'Your harvest's aftergrowth you shall not reap, and your grapes of untrimmed vines you shall not gather; <u>the land shall have a sabbatical year</u>.
(Leviticus 25:1-5)

Apparently, Israel ignored this law about giving the land a sabbatical rest every seven years for 490 years. Four-hundred ninety years divided by seven (since they were supposed to let it rest every seven) equals seventy years. Over the course of 490 years, the land was supposed to rest one year, every seven years for a total of 70 years. They had not obeyed, so they owed God 70 years of letting the land rest. God took them out of the land for 70 years, to force the land to rest. After 490 years of disobedience came 70 years of punishment. Then, Daniel received a 490 year prophesy from Gabriel in Daniel 9:24-27.

The 490 year prophesy is broken up into segments. The first segment is "Seven sets of seven plus sixty-two sets of seven" (Daniel 9:25 NLT), or 483 years. The 483 years start "from the time the command is given to rebuild Jerusalem" (Daniel 9:25 NLT) and end with "the Anointed One" or the Messiah. The 483 years were started in Nehemiah 2 before the wall of Jerusalem was built, and ended with the triumphal entry in Matthew 21.

The second segment of the prophesy takes place "after this period of sixty-two sets of seven" (Daniel 9:26 NLT). After the triumphal entry on Palm Sunday, Jesus was killed a few days later, appearing to have not been the king they were hoping for.

In 70 A.D., a few decades after the Anointed One died, the temple in Jerusalem was destroyed.

> 26 "After this period of sixty-two sets of seven, the Anointed One will be killed, appearing to have accomplished nothing, and a ruler will arise whose armies will destroy the city and the Temple. The end will come with a flood, and war and its miseries are decreed from that time to the very end. (Daniel 9:26 NLT)

The "flood," and "war" at the "very end", are future events described in Revelation 12:14-17:

> 14 But the two wings of the great eagle were given to the woman, so that she could fly into the wilderness to her place, where she was nourished for a time and times and half a time, from the presence of the serpent.
> 15 And the serpent poured water like a river out of his mouth after the woman, so that he might cause her to be swept away with the flood.
> 16 But the earth helped the woman, and the earth opened its mouth and drank up the river which the dragon poured out of his mouth.
> 17 So the dragon was enraged with the woman, and went off to make war with the rest of her children, who keep the commandments of God and hold to the testimony of Jesus. (Revelation 12:14-17)

The woman in Revelation 12 symbolizes Israel. Only Israel fits with all four descriptions given about the woman. First, the sign of the sun, moon, and 12 stars match the signs of the patriarchs of Israel in Joseph's dream in Genesis 37:9-10. Second, "And she gave birth to a son, a male *child*, who is to rule all the nations with a rod of iron; and her child was caught up to God and to His throne" (Revelation 12:5). The child is, of course, Jesus, and as Mary gave birth to Jesus, He was also one of the children of Israel. Third, the woman was to "fly into the wilderness" for "a time and times and half a time" in Revelation 12:14. "Time" means one year, "times" means two years, and "half of times" means half a year, for a total of three and a half years that the woman is supposed to be in the wilderness. This fits with Jesus instruction for those in Judea to "flee to the mountains" after the ABOMINATION OF DESOLATION which was spoken of through Daniel the prophet".

> 15 "Therefore when you see the ABOMINATION OF DESOLATION which was spoken of through Daniel the prophet, standing in the holy place (let the reader understand),
> 16 then those who are in <u>Judea must flee to the mountains</u>. (Matthew 24:15-16)

Finally, the woman in Revelation 12 is Israel because she has "children, who keep the commandments of God and hold to the testimony of Jesus." (Revelation 12:17) Those who hold to the testimony of Jesus are Christians. Christians are the spiritual decedents of Abraham, the father of faith, who is the father of Israel.

> 16 For this reason *it is* <u>by faith</u>, in order that *it may be* in accordance with grace, so that the promise will be guaranteed to <u>all the descendants</u>, not only to those who are of the Law, but also to those <u>who</u>

are of the faith of Abraham, who is the father of us all, (Romans 4:16)

Only Israel meets the requirements of being the sun, moon, and 12 stars, giving birth to Jesus, needing to flee to the wilderness, and having children who "hold to the testimony of Jesus."

My tangent about the woman in Revelation 12 has two purposes. First, it matched the "flood" and "war" at the "very end" from Daniel 9:26. Second, it introduced the "ABOMINATION OF DESOLATION which was spoken of through Daniel the prophet" from Matthew 24:15, which is referring to Daniel 9:27, Daniel 11:31, and Daniel 12:11.

Back to Daniel's seventy sevens (490 years) prophesy from Daniel 9:24-27. The final set of seven years is a future event called Daniel's 70th seven, Daniel's 70th week, the seven year tribulation, or simply the tribulation. Remember the prophesy was broken up into segments. First, the 483 years in Daniel 9:25, then what takes place after the 483 years in Daniel 9:26, and finally the last seven years of the prophesy in Daniel 9:27. There is a significant gap between the first 483 years and the last seven years of the 490-year prophesy. We find a similar gap in other prophesies about Jesus. For example, Jesus fulfilled Isaiah's prophesy:

> 16 And He came to Nazareth, where He had been brought up; and as was His custom, He entered the synagogue on the Sabbath, and stood up to read.
> 17 And the book of the prophet Isaiah was handed to Him. And He opened the book and found the place where it was written,
> 18 "THE SPIRIT OF THE LORD IS UPON ME, BECAUSE HE ANOINTED ME TO PREACH THE GOSPEL TO THE POOR.

He has sent Me to proclaim release to the captives, And recovery of sight to the blind, To set free those who are oppressed,

19 To proclaim the favorable year of the Lord."

20 And He closed the book, gave it back to the attendant and sat down; and the eyes of all in the synagogue were fixed on Him.

21 And He began to say to them, "Today this Scripture has been fulfilled in your hearing." (Luke 4:16-21)

It becomes quite interesting when you go back and find for yourself the passage Jesus found, and consider where Jesus stopped reading.

1 The Spirit of the Lord God is upon me,
Because the Lord has anointed me
To bring good news to the afflicted;
He has sent me to bind up the brokenhearted,
To proclaim liberty to captives
And freedom to prisoners;
2 To proclaim the favorable year of the Lord
And the day of vengeance of our God;
To comfort all who mourn,
3 To grant those who mourn *in* Zion,
Giving them a garland instead of ashes,
The oil of gladness instead of mourning,
The mantle of praise instead of a spirit of fainting.
So they will be called oaks of righteousness,
The planting of the Lord, that He may be
glorified. (Isaiah 61:1-3)

He stopped reading and closed the scroll in the middle of a sentence. While Jesus fulfilled Isaiah 61:1-2a in His first coming, the latter part of Isaiah 61:2 and the rest of the passage will not be fulfilled until His second coming. Isaiah 61 illustrates there is precedence for gaps in messianic prophesies, so the gap before Daniel 9:27 should not be of concern.

> [27] The ruler will make a treaty with the people for a period of one set of seven, but after half this time, he will put an end to the sacrifices and offerings. And as a climax to all his terrible deeds, he will set up a sacrilegious object that causes desecration, until the fate decreed for this defiler is finally poured out on him." (Daniel 9:27 NLT)

We are told Daniel's 70th seven starts with a seven year treaty. However, after half of those seven years, everything goes awry. After three-and-a-half years a "sacrilegious object that causes desecration" is set up in the future temple. Jesus calls this the "ABOMINATION OF DESOLATION" in Matthew 24:15-16, when those in Judea are to "flee to the mountains" or wilderness (Revelation 12:14) for three and a half years. The end of Daniel's seventieth seven, and the end of all the seventy sevens will bring an end to sin.

> 24 "A period of seventy sets of seven has been decreed for your people and your holy city to finish their rebellion, to put an end to their sin, to atone for their guilt, to bring in everlasting righteousness, to confirm the prophetic vision, and to anoint the Most Holy Place. (Daniel 9:24 NLT)

We examined Leviticus 25, 2 Chronicles 36, Isaiah 61, Daniel 9, Matthew 24, Luke 4, Romans 4, and Revelation 12 all to show there is a future seven year tribulation. The Pre-Tribulation rapture view places the rapture before this seven year tribulation.

Another major point of the Pre-Tribulation view is that the rapture will take place before the "wrath of God."

> 10 and to wait for His Son from heaven, whom He raised from the dead, *that is* Jesus, who rescues us from the wrath to come. (1 Thessalonians 1:10)

> 9 For God has not destined us for wrath, but for obtaining salvation through our Lord Jesus Christ, (1 Thessalonians 5:9)

Pre-Tribulationalists see the entire seven year tribulation as "wrath," therefore requiring that the rapture come before Daniel's seventieth seven.

Most Pre-Tribulationalists interpret Revelation 4-19 to be Daniel's seventieth seven, and infer that the rapture takes place at or before Revelation 4:1.

> 1 After these things I looked, and behold, a door *standing* open in heaven, and the first voice which I had heard, like *the sound* of a trumpet speaking with me, said, "Come up here, and I will show you what must take place after these things." (Revelation 4:1)

In the context of Revelation 4:1, Pre-Tribulationalist J. Vernon McGee writes, "This is a definite statement concerning the Rapture." (*Thru the Bible with J. Vernon McGee*, page 929).

Many who hold to the Pre-Tribulation rapture defend the view with Revelation 3:10. They take the phrase "keep you from" to mean "rapture you out", and "hour of testing" to mean the seven year tribulation.

> 10 'Because you have kept the word of My perseverance, I also will <u>keep you from</u> the <u>hour of testing</u>, that *hour* which is about to come upon the whole world, to test those who dwell on the earth. (Revelation 3:10)

Another common defense is to note the word "church" is used many times in Revelation 1-3, but is not used in Revelation 4-19.

The Pre-Tribulation view sees John 14:1-4 as Jesus taking raptured believers to His Father's House for the seven year tribulation.

> 1 "Do not let your heart be troubled; believe in God, believe also in Me.
> 2 "In My Father's house are many dwelling places; if it were not so, I would have told you; for I go to prepare a place for you.
> 3 "If I go and prepare a place for you, <u>I will come again and receive you to Myself, that where I am, *there* you may be also.</u>
> 4 "And you know the way where I am going." (John 14:1-4)

Also, Pre-Tribulationalists believe the rapture is imminent. They think the rapture can happen at any time. One verse that might be used to defend this is:

> 7 "And behold, <u>I am coming quickly</u>. Blessed is he who heeds the words of the prophecy of this book." (Revelation 22:7)

Finally, some Pre-Tribulationalists argue that Jesus would not allow His "bride" to go through the seven year tribulation, and therefore the rapture must be before the tribulation. 2 Corinthians 11:2 describes a church as being betrothed to Christ, in other words the bride of Christ.

> For I am jealous for you with a godly jealousy; for I <u>betrothed</u> you to one husband, so that to <u>Christ</u> I might present you *as* a pure virgin. (2 Corinthians 11:2)

To summarize the main points of the Pre-Tribulation view:

1. There will be a future seven year tribulation (Daniel 9:27).

2. The rapture will take place before the wrath of God (1 Thessalonians 5:9).

3. The rapture will take place before the seven year tribulation (Revelation 3:10).

4. The word "church" is used in Revelation 1-3, but not Revelation 4-19 (Revelation 1-19).

5. The rapture takes place at or before Revelation 4:1 (Revelation 4:1).

6. Jesus will take raptured believers to His Father's House for the seven year tribulation (John 14:1-4).

7. Two resurrections/raptures of believers are needed, one before and one after the seven year tribulation (Revelation 20:4).

8. The rapture is imminent (Revelation 22:7).

9. Jesus would not allow His Bride to be treated that way (2 Corinthians 11:2).

Mid-Tribulation Pre-Millennial View

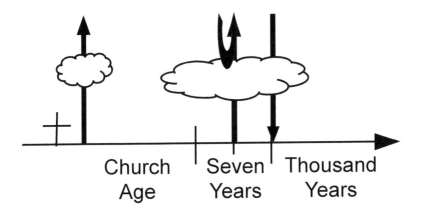

| Church | Seven | Thousand |
| Age | Years | Years |

The Mid-Tribulation view is that the rapture will take place in the middle of the seven year tribulation.

The order of events needed for the Mid-Tribulation view:

1. Three and a Half Years of Tribulation (Daniel 9:27)

2. Resurrection (1 Thessalonians 4:16)

3. Rapture (1 Thessalonians 4:17)

4. Three and a Half Years of Tribulation (Daniel 9:27)

5. Another Resurrection (Revelation 20:4)

6. Another Rapture (Matthew 24:29-31)

7. 2nd Coming (Hebrews 9:28)

8. 1,000 year reign (Revelation 20:4-6)

9. 2nd Death (Revelation 20:11-15)

The Mid-Tribulation view has some similarities to the Pre-Trib view, but instead of the rapture being before Daniel's 70th seven, it is in the middle of Daniel's 70th seven, corresponding to the Abomination of Desolation.

> 27 The ruler will make a treaty with the people for a period of <u>one set of seven</u>, but <u>after half this time</u>, he will put an end to the sacrifices and offerings. And as a climax to all his terrible deeds, he will set up a sacrilegious object that causes <u>desecration</u>, until the fate decreed for this defiler is finally poured out on him." (Daniel 9:27 NLT)

Below are the main points of the Mid-Tribulation view:

1. Rapture at the seventh trumpet (1 Corinthians 15:51-52, Revelation 11:15-17)

2. Seven trumpets start before the middle of the tribulation (Revelation 8-11)

3. There will be a future seven year tribulation (Daniel 9:27)

4. The Rapture will take place in the middle of the tribulation (2 Thessalonians 2:1-4)

5. The rapture will take place before the wrath of God (1 Thessalonians 5:9)

6. Jesus will take raptured believers to His Father's House for the last three and a half years of tribulation. (John 14:1-4)

7. Two resurrections/raptures of believers are needed, one before and one after the last three and a half years of tribulation. (Revelation 20:4)

Rapture at the seventh trumpet (1 Corinthians 15:51-52, Revelation 11:15-17)

Mid-Tribulationalists place the seventh trumpet of Revelation in the middle of the tribulation, and therefore place the rapture at the seventh trumpet. Trumpets play an important role in the rapture event, which is emphasized by its repeated use in the rapture passages:

> 31 "And He will send forth His angels with A GREAT TRUMPET and THEY WILL GATHER TOGETHER His elect from the four winds, from one end of the sky to the other. (Matthew 24:31)

> 16 For the Lord Himself will descend from heaven with a shout, with the voice of *the* archangel and with the trumpet of God, and the dead in Christ will rise first.
> 17 Then we who are alive and remain will be caught up together with them in the clouds to meet the Lord in the air, and so we shall always be with the Lord. (1 Thessalonians 4:16-17)

> 51 Behold, I tell you a mystery; we will not all sleep, but we will all be changed,
> 52 in a moment, in the twinkling of an eye, at the

last trumpet; for the trumpet will sound, and the dead will be raised imperishable, and we will be changed. (1 Corinthians 15:51-52)

From the three rapture passages above, we see the trumpet signals that the elect will be gathered in the sky or "caught up in the air," and those who had not physically died ("we will not all sleep") will be changed. It will be a great trumpet of God, and it will be the last. Notice in the Matthew passage "A GREAT TRUMPET" is in all caps. This means the translators are pointing us back to Old Testament passages such as Isaiah 27:13 and Zechariah 9:14.

> 12 In that day the LORD will start *His* threshing from the flowing stream of the Euphrates to the brook of Egypt, and you will be gathered up one by one, O sons of Israel.
> 13 It will come about also in that day that a great trumpet will be blown, and those who were perishing in the land of Assyria and who were scattered in the land of Egypt will come and worship the LORD in the holy mountain at Jerusalem. (Isaiah 27:12-13)

> 14 Then the LORD will appear over them,
> And His arrow will go forth like lightning;
> And the Lord GOD will blow the trumpet,
> And will march in the storm winds of the south.
> 15 The LORD of hosts will defend them.
> And they will devour and trample on the sling stones;
> And they will drink *and* be boisterous as with wine;

44

And they will be filled like a *sacrificial* basin,
Drenched like the corners of the altar.
16 And the LORD their <u>God will save them in that day</u>
As the flock of His people;
For *they are as* the stones of a crown,
Sparkling in His land. (Zechariah 9:14-16)

The passage from 1 Corinthians provides another interesting detail about "the last trumpet." It turns out there are seven trumpets in Revelation. Before the seventh and last trumpet is blown, it is said:

> 7 but in the days of the voice of the <u>seventh</u> angel, when he is about to sound, then the <u>mystery of God is finished</u>, as He preached to His servants the prophets. (Revelation 10:7)

Mid-Tribulationalist James Oliver Buswell Jr., wrote:

> "I suggest that the statement that the mystery of God is finished is at the sounding of the seventh trumpet, is an indication that the rapture of the church takes place at that point." (Buswell, *A Systematic Theology of the Christian Religion, Volume 2*, page 450)

When we look at the point the seventh trumpet is blown, it is announced the kingdom has come, which seems an appropriate time for the rapture. Then, when coupled with the fact that the seventh trumpet in Revelation is the last trumpet, it is easy to see the connection to the change in our bodies that takes place at the rapture described in 1 Corinthians 15:51-52.

51 Behold, I tell you a mystery; we will not all sleep, but <u>we will all be changed</u>,
52 in a moment, in the twinkling of an eye, at the <u>last trumpet</u>; for the <u>trumpet</u> will sound, and the <u>dead will be raised imperishable</u>, and <u>we will be changed</u>. (1 Corinthians 15:51-52)

15 Then the <u>seventh angel sounded</u>; and there were loud voices in heaven, saying, <u>"The kingdom of the world has become *the kingdom* of our Lord and of His Christ</u>; and He will reign forever and ever." (Revelation 11:15)

Buswell wrote:

> "Now is identified the moment toward which we look when we use the words of the Lord's prayer, 'Thy kingdom come, Thy will be done on earth as it is in heaven.'" (Buswell, *A Systematic Theology of the Christian Religion, Volume 2*, page 457)

The trumpet thread is woven throughout prophetic scripture, and culminates in the last trumpet, completing the "mystery." The mystery is what was not completely revealed in the Old Testament, in this case that "we will not all sleep, but we will all be changed … at the last trumpet" (1 Corinthians 15:51-52).

Seven trumpets start before the middle of the tribulation (Revelation 8-11)

By logical deduction, since the Mid-Tribulationalists place the seventh trumpet at the middle of the tribulation, that means all seven trumpets (Revelation 8-11) are blown by the middle of the tribulation.

There will be a future seven year tribulation (Daniel 9:27)

This is a similar position held by Pre-Tribulationalists. The difference being, the Mid-Tribulationalists place the rapture in the middle of the seven years, and the Pre-Tribulatialists place the rapture at the beginning of the seven years.

The rapture will take place in the middle of the tribulation (2 Thessalonians 2:1-4)

This point is where the view gets its name. There is definitely a significance to the middle of the tribulation. The three and a half years are referred to in various ways: half of the set of seven (Daniel 9:27), time, times, and half a time (Daniel 7:25, 12:7, Revelation 12:14), 1,290 days (Daniel 12:11), 42 months (Revelation 11:2, 13:5), and 1,260 days (Revelation 11:3, 12:6). The beast from the earth was given 42 months of authority.

> 4 they worshiped the dragon because he gave his authority to the beast; and they worshiped the beast, saying, "Who is like the beast, and who is able to wage war with him?"
> 5 There was given to him a mouth speaking arrogant words and blasphemies, and authority to act for forty-two months was given to him.
> (Revelation 13:4-5)

The Mid-Tribulation view places the rapture at the time when people start worshiping the beast, in the middle of Daniel's 70th seven.

1 Now we request you, brethren, with regard to the coming of our Lord Jesus Christ and <u>our gathering together to Him</u>,

2 that you not be quickly shaken from your composure or be disturbed either by a spirit or a message or a letter as if from us, to the effect that the day of the Lord has come.

3 Let no one in any way deceive you, for <u>*it will not come*</u> <u>unless</u> the apostasy comes first, and <u>the man of lawlessness is revealed</u>, the son of destruction,

4 who opposes and <u>exalts himself above every so-called god or object of worship</u>, so that he takes his <u>seat in the temple of God</u>, displaying himself <u>as being God</u>. (2 Thessalonians 2:1-4)

The rapture will take place before the wrath of God (1 Thessalonians 5:9)

While in agreement with the Pre-Tribulation view that the rapture will take place before God's wrath, the definition of when God's wrath starts is different. From the Mid-Tribulationalists view, only the bowls contain the wrath believers are not destined for.

9 For God has <u>not destined us for wrath</u>, but for obtaining salvation through our Lord Jesus Christ, (1 Thessalonians 5:9)

1 Then I heard a loud voice from the temple, saying to the seven angels, "Go and pour out on

the earth <u>the seven bowls of the wrath of God</u>."
(Revelation 16:1)

Mid-Tribulationalists do not see the seven seals and the seven trumpets as wrath.

Jesus will take raptured believers to His Father's House for the last three and a half years of tribulation. (John 14:1-4)

Similar to the Pre-Tribulation view, Mid-Tribulationalists believe raptured believers will spend time in heaven between the rapture and the second coming. In the Mid-Tribulation case, three and a half years will be spent in heaven.

Two resurrections/raptures of believers are needed, one before and one after the last three and a half years of tribulation. (Revelation 20:4)

This point is very similar to the Pre-Tribulation view. Both views require a rapture and resurrection, followed by a period of time where more people can come to Christ. Those new believers will need imperishable bodies, so another rapture and resurrection are needed.

> 42 So also is the <u>resurrection</u> of the dead. It is sown a perishable *body*, it is <u>raised an imperishable *body*;</u> *(*1 Corinthians 15:42)

One passage that can be used to show there are believers in the last three and a half years of the tribulation is Revelation 12.

> 14 But the two wings of the great eagle were given to the woman, so that she could fly into the wilderness to her place, where she was nourished

for a <u>time and times and half a time</u>, from the presence of the <u>serpent</u>. (Revelation 12:14)

17 So the <u>dragon</u> was enraged with the woman, and went off to make war with the rest of her children, who keep the commandments of God and <u>hold to the testimony of Jesus</u>. (Revelation 12:17)

While those from Judea flee to the wilderness for three and a half years (time, times, and half of times) the dragon is making war with the Christians (those "who hold to the testimony of Jesus"). Therefore, those "who hold to the testimony of Jesus" and survive the last half of the tribulation, will need to be raptured at the end of the tribulation.

Pre-Wrath Pre-Millennial View

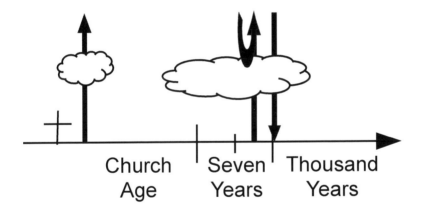

Church Age   Seven Years   Thousand Years

The Pre-wrath view is that the rapture will take place during the latter half of the seven year tribulation, between the sixth and seventh seals. This view sees the wrath of God as starting after the sixth seal, and holds that the rapture will be before the wrath, hence the name Pre-Wrath.

The order of events needed for the Pre-Wrath view:

1. Three and a Half Years of Tribulation (Daniel 9:27)

2. More Tribulation, Less than Three Years and One Month (Matthew 24:15-29)

3. Resurrection (1 Thessalonians 4:16)

4. Rapture (1 Thessalonians 4:17)

5. At least Five More Months of Tribulation (Revelation 9:5)

6. 2nd Coming (Hebrews 9:28)

7. 1,000 year reign (Revelation 20:4-6)

8. 2nd Death (Revelation 20:11-15)

The Pre-Wrath view is similar to the Mid-Trib view, but instead of the rapture being at the halfway point of Daniel's 70th seven, it is past the middle, but at least five months before the end, corresponding to the sixth seal of Revelation 6, and the great multitude of Revelation 7.

> 12 I looked when He broke the sixth seal, and there was a great earthquake; and the sun became black as sackcloth *made* of hair, and the whole moon became like blood;
> 13 and the stars of the sky fell to the earth, as a fig tree casts its unripe figs when shaken by a great wind.
> 14 The sky was split apart like a scroll when it is rolled up, and every mountain and island were moved out of their places.
> 15 Then the kings of the earth and the great men and the commanders and the rich and the strong and every slave and free man hid themselves in the caves and among the rocks of the mountains;
> 16 and they said to the mountains and to the

rocks, "Fall on us and hide us from the presence of Him who sits on the throne, and from the wrath of the Lamb;

17 for the great day of their wrath has come, and who is able to stand?" (Revelation 6:12-17)

9 After these things I looked, and behold, a great multitude which no one could count, from every nation and *all* tribes and peoples and tongues, standing before the throne and before the Lamb, clothed in white robes, and palm branches *were* in their hands; (Revelation 7:9)

The Pre-Wrath view places the rapture after the middle of the tribulation, because the middle of the tribulation occurs at verse 15 of Matthew 24, and they believe the rapture takes place at verse 31 of Matthew 24, 16 verses after the middle. While it is difficult to pinpoint how long it takes those 16 verses to unfold, they conclude the rapture is at least after the middle of the seven year tribulation.

15 "Therefore when you see the ABOMINATION OF DESOLATION which was spoken of through Daniel the prophet, standing in the holy place (let the reader understand), (Matthew 24:15)

31 "And He will send forth His angels with A GREAT TRUMPET and THEY WILL GATHER TOGETHER His elect from the four winds, from one end of the sky to the other. (Matthew 24:31)

The Pre-Wrath view also places the seven trumpets after the rapture. Since the fifth trumpet has a five-month duration, they can conclude the rapture is at least five months before the end of the seven year tribulation. This allows for the rapture to fall into a three year window, from three years seven months, to six years seven months into the seven year tribulation.

> 5 And they were not permitted to kill anyone, but to torment for <u>five months</u>; and their torment was like the torment of a scorpion when it stings a man. (Revelation 9:5)

Since we know there will be believers on the earth for at least part of the last three and a half years (Revelation 13:5-8), and the Pre-Tribulation and Mid-Tribulation views place the rapture at or before the middle of the tribulation, those views require a second rapture (Matthew 24:31) for those who come to Christ in the last half of the seven year tribulation. However, the Pre-Wrath view has the rapture in the last half of the seven year tribulation. Furthermore, they hold that the Matthew 24:31 rapture is the first and only rapture. For the Pre-Wrath view to only have one rapture, it does require the 144,000 who have the "seal of God" (Revelation 9:4) to not be raptured, since Pre-Wrathers would have them on earth after the rapture.

> 5 There was given to him a mouth speaking arrogant words and blasphemies, and authority to act for <u>forty-two months</u> was given to him.
> 6 And he opened his mouth in blasphemies against God, to blaspheme His name and His tabernacle, *that is*, those who dwell in heaven.
> 7 It was also given to him <u>to make war with the saints</u> and to overcome them, and authority over every tribe and people and tongue and nation was given to him. (Revelation 13:5-7)

Below are the main points of the Pre-Wrath view:

1. 6th seal celestial disturbances match Jesus' rapture prerequisites. (Revelation 6:12-14, Matthew 24:29-31)

2. Wrath of God starts after the 6th seal is opened. (Revelation 6:15-17)

3. Jesus will take raptured believers to His Father's House for at least the last five months of the tribulation. (John 14:1-4)

6th seal celestial disturbances match Jesus' rapture prerequisites (Revelation 6:12-14, Matthew 24:29-31)

There is a very close parallel between Matthew 24, Mark 13, Luke 21, and Revelation 6. Often John gets left out in the harmony of the Gospels, but in this case he provides a parallel account. In the case of the Gospels Jesus is telling four of the apostles (Peter, James, John, and Andrew (Mark 13:3)) about the signs of the second coming. In Revelation 6, we are told of the effects of Jesus removing the seals to the scroll.

Harmony of the gospel writers at a glance:

	Matthew	Mark	Luke	Revelation
1st Seal – False Christ	24:3-5	13:4-6	21:7-8	6:1-2
2nd Seal – Wars	24:6	13:7	21:9-10	6:3-4
3rd Seal – Famine	24:7	13:8	21:11	6:5-6
4th Seal – Death	24:7	13:8	21:11	6:7-8
5th Seal – Martyrs	24:9-28	13:9-23	21:12-24	6:9-11
6th Seal – Sky Falling	24:29-31	13:24-27	21:25-28	6:12-17

I suggest you read Matthew 24:3-31 and Revelation 6 with this table in hand and identify the similarities. The celestial disturbances in the 6th seal, and those that precede the gathering of the elect in Matthew 24:29-31 are extremely similar. This similarity is the basis for the timing of the Pre-Wrath view.

Below is a portion of the two passages in parallel, to help highlight their similarities.

29 "But immediately after the tribulation of those days THE SUN WILL BE DARKENED, AND THE MOON WILL NOT GIVE ITS LIGHT, AND THE STARS WILL FALL from the sky, and the powers of the heavens will be shaken. 30 "And then the sign of the Son of Man will appear in the sky, and then all the tribes of the earth will mourn, and they will see the SON OF MAN COMING ON THE CLOUDS OF THE SKY with power and great glory. 31 "And He will send forth His angels with A GREAT TRUMPET and THEY WILL GATHER TOGETHER His elect from the four winds, from one end of the sky to the other. (Matthew 24:29-31)	12 I looked when He broke the sixth seal, and there was a great earthquake; and the sun became black as sackcloth *made* of hair, and the whole moon became like blood; 13 and the stars of the sky fell to the earth, as a fig tree casts its unripe figs when shaken by a great wind. 14 The sky was split apart like a scroll when it is rolled up, and every mountain and island were moved out of their places. 15 Then the kings of the earth and the great men and the commanders and the rich and the strong and every slave and free man hid themselves in the caves and among the rocks of the mountains; 16 and they said to the mountains and to the rocks, "Fall on us and hide us from the presence of Him who sits on the throne, and from the wrath of the Lamb; 17 for the great day of their wrath has come, and who is able to stand?" (Revelation 6:12-17)

The sun and moon darkened are the prerequisites for the Day of the Lord.

> 31 "The sun will be turned into darkness
> And the moon into blood
> Before the great and awesome day of the Lord
> comes. (Joel 2:31)

Those cosmic disturbances take place at the 6th seal:

> 12 I looked when He broke the sixth seal, and
> there was a great earthquake; and the sun became
> black as sackcloth made of hair, and the whole
> moon became like blood; (Revelation 6:12)

Furthermore, Jesus returns at that same time as described in the Olivet Discourse:

> 29 "But immediately after the tribulation of those
> days the sun will be darkened, and the moon will
> not give its light, and the stars will fall from the
> sky, and the powers of the heavens will be shaken.
> 30 "And then the sign of the Son of Man will
> appear in the sky, and then all the tribes of the
> earth will mourn, and they will see the Son of
> Man coming on the clouds of the sky with power
> and great glory.
> 31 "And He will send forth His angels with a great
> trumpet and they will gather together His elect
> from the four winds, from one end of the sky to
> the other. (Matthew 24:29-31)

Therefore, the Day of the Lord starts when the sixth seal is opened (Revelation 6:12-17), when the sun is darkened, and the moon turns to blood (Joel 2:31). It is the coming of the Lord (Matthew 24:29-31).

Wrath of God starts after the 6th seal is opened (Revelation 6:15-17)

While in agreement with the Pre-Tribulation, and Mid-Tribulation views that the rapture will take place before God's wrath, the definition of when God's wrath starts is different. From the Pre-Wrath view the wrath of God starts after the sixth seal is broken. The seventh seal, the seven trumpets, and the seven bowls are all considered wrath. This is taken from Revelation 6:16-17:

> 16 and they said to the mountains and to the rocks, "Fall on us and hide us from the presence of Him who sits on the throne, and from the wrath of the Lamb;
> 17 for the great day of their wrath has come, and who is able to stand?" (Revelation 6:16-17)

It is from this point that the view gets its name Pre-Wrath. Revelation 6:16 is the first verse in Revelation that uses the word wrath. While bad things happened on earth during the first five seals, they were not the wrath of God. They were just tribulation. Wrath and tribulation are different words with different meanings. Wrath is more severe and has a connotation of anger. Tribulation is a lesser kind of trouble. Christians are expected to face tribulation, but not the wrath of God.

Jesus will take raptured believers to His Father's House for at least the last five months of the tribulation. (John 14:1-4)

Similar to the Pre-Trib and Mid-Trib views, the Pre-Wrath view sees raptured believers spending time in heaven before the second coming. At a minimum, this would be five months since the 5th trumpet lasts five months, and the Pre-Wrath view places the 5th trumpet (all the trumpets) between the rapture and the second coming.

> 5 And they were not permitted to kill anyone, but to torment for <u>five months</u>; and their torment was like the torment of a scorpion when it stings a man. (Revelation 9:5)

At a maximum the raptured believers would spend three and a half years in the Father's house before returning to earth with Christ. This is due to the gathering in Matthew 24:31, following the Abomination of Desolation in the middle of the seven years, found in Matthew 24:15.

> 15 "Therefore when you see the <u>ABOMINATION OF DESOLATION</u> which was spoken of through Daniel the prophet, standing in the holy place (let the reader understand), (Matthew 24:15)

> 31 "And He will send forth His angels with A GREAT TRUMPET and THEY WILL <u>GATHER TOGETHER</u> His elect from the four winds, from one end of the sky to the other. (Matthew 24:31)

Post-Tribulation Pre-Millennial View

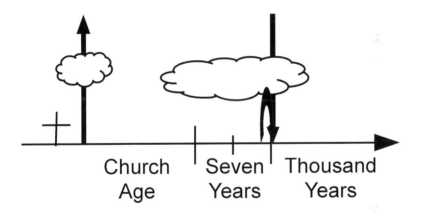

| Church Age | Seven Years | Thousand Years |

The Post-Tribulation view is that the rapture will take place at the end of, or after the seven year tribulation. This view sees the wrath of God as starting with the seven bowls of God's wrath. Some Post-Tribulationalists hold that the rapture will take place before the bowls are poured out. The bowls could be poured out in a very short amount of time, maybe just half an hour, as there are no time restrictions in any of the descriptions of the seven bowls.

The order of events needed for the Post-Tribulation view:

1. Seven Years of Tribulation (Daniel 9:27)

2. Resurrection (1 Thessalonians 4:16)

3. Rapture (1 Thessalonians 4:17)

4. 2nd Coming (Hebrews 9:28)

5. 1,000 year reign (Revelation 20:4-6)

6. 2nd Death (Revelation 20:11-15)

There are several varieties of the Post-Tribulation view. There are several reasons for the variety. First, the view has been around far longer than any of the other Pre-Millennial views. It is for this reason that the Post-Tribulational Pre-Millennial view is often referred to as Historic Pre-Millennialism[2]. Nearly two millennia allowed for more divergence in the view. Second, since the focus of the Post-Tribulation view is on the end of the tribulation, the rest of the tribulation is left more open for debate. Finally, the Post-Tribulation Pre-Millennial view is most similar to the A-Millennial and Post-Millennial structures, since they all have only one future coming of Jesus. So, there is a chance for blending between the millennial views. The same is true in regards to Futurists, Partial-Preterists, Historicists, and Idealists, whom can all hold to the Post-Tribulation view, and share ideas and create variety in the Post-Tribulation framework. For the above reasons, I am only going to include three essentials of the Post-Trib view:

---

2 The term "Historic Pre-Millennial" should not be confused with "Historicist Pre-Millennial." "Historic Pre-Millennial" usually means "Futurist Post-Trib Pre-Millennial," because historically that used to be the only Pre-Millennial view. It is also known as Classical Pre-Millennialism for the same reasons.

1. Only one second-coming (Hebrews 9:28)
2. Only one first resurrection (Revelation 20:4-6)
3. The rapture will take place before the wrath of God (1 Thessalonians 5:9)

Only one second-coming (Hebrews 9:28)

Part of the essence of the Post-Trib view is seeing that the resurrection, rapture, wrath, second coming, Har-Magedon (Armageddon), and the day of the Lord are all elements of the same event. The rapture is not separated from the second coming by years, or months (as is the case with the other Pre-Millennial views). With the Post-Tribulation view they are part of the same event. As Jesus is returning, those resurrected (1 Thessalonians 4:16) and raptured are caught up to meet Him in the clouds (1 Thessalonians 4:17). During the reunion in the clouds the bowls of wrath are poured out (Revelation 16). Then, Christ accompanied by the redeemed continues on His way down to do battle (Revelation 19:11-21), and usher in the "great and terrible day of the LORD" (Malachi 4:5). This is the second coming spoken of in Hebrews, and alluded to in Acts.

> 28 so Christ also, having been offered once to bear the sins of many, will appear a second time for salvation without *reference to* sin, to those who eagerly await Him. (Hebrews 9:28)

> 11 They also said, "Men of Galilee, why do you stand looking into the sky? This Jesus, who has been taken up from you into heaven, will come in just the same way as you have watched Him go into heaven." (Acts 1:11)

According to the Post-Tribulation view, Jesus went up once, and will come back down once. On His way down, the resurrected and raptured will meet Him in the air.

> 17 Then we who are alive and remain will be caught up together with them in the clouds to <u>meet the Lord in the air</u>, and so we shall always be with the Lord. (1 Thessalonians 4:17)

This custom of meeting was illustrated by the father of the prodigal son (Luke 15:11-32). When the father saw him, he ran to meet the son and returned back home with him. This type of meeting was also done for Paul. When the church in Rome heard Paul was on his way, they went out to meet him, and Paul returned with them. In a similar way, Post-Tribulationalists believe that when Jesus returns, those raptured will meet Him in the clouds, and return back to earth with Him.

> 14 There we found *some* brethren, and were invited to stay with them for seven days; and thus we came to <u>Rome</u>.
> 15 And the brethren, when they heard about us, came from there as far as the Market of Appius and Three Inns <u>to meet us</u>; and when Paul saw them, he thanked God and took courage.
> 16 <u>When we entered Rome</u>, Paul was allowed to stay by himself, with the soldier who was guarding him. (Acts 28:14-16)

Only one first resurrection (Revelation 20:4-6)

> 4 Then I saw thrones, and they sat on them, and judgment was given to them. And I *saw* the <u>souls</u>

of those who had been beheaded because of their
testimony of Jesus and because of the word of
God, and those who had not worshiped the beast
or his image, and had not received the mark on
their forehead and on their hand; and they came
to life and reigned with Christ for a thousand
years.
5 The rest of the dead did not come to life until the
thousand years were completed. This is the first
resurrection.
6 Blessed and holy is the one who has a part in the
first resurrection; over these the second death has
no power, but they will be priests of God and of
Christ and will reign with Him for a thousand
years. (Revelation 20:4-6)

The Pre-Millennial passage Revelation 20:4-6, informs the
readers there is a "first resurrection", and a "second death." The
first resurrection is for followers of Christ, the second death is
for those whose names were not written in the Lambs book of
life.

14 Then death and Hades were thrown into the
lake of fire. This is the second death, the lake of
fire.
15 And if anyone's name was not found written in
the book of life, he was thrown into the lake of
fire. (Revelation 20:14-15)

The first resurrection precedes the 1,000 year reign with Christ.
From the Post-Tribulationalists perspective, there is only one
first resurrection at the end of the tribulation, with the second

coming of Christ, before the 1,000 year reign begins. The first resurrection is part of the second coming event.

From 1 Corinthians 15:22-24, we learn there is an order to the resurrection, first there was Christ in the first century, then there will be a resurrection of those who are Christ's when He comes back. Only one resurrection event is listed for those who are Christ's, then comes the end.

> 22 For as in Adam all die, so also in Christ all will be <u>made alive</u>.
> 23 But each in his own <u>order</u>: <u>Christ the first fruits,</u> after that <u>those who are Christ's at His coming,</u> <u>24 then *comes* the end,</u> when He hands over the kingdom to the God and Father, when He has abolished all rule and all authority and power. (1 Corinthians 15:22-24)

To further clarify, there are several types of "resurrections." First, some have been raised from the dead by either miracles (e.g. Lazarus), cardiopulmonary resuscitation (CPR), or other ways a dead person can come back to life. Merely coming back to life is not what these passages are referring to, we know this because Jesus was not the "the first fruits" of that type of resurrection. The second type of resurrection was Jesus' resurrection, where He received a glorified body. This is called "the first fruits," meaning He was the first to receive this type of resurrection with a glorified body. Then, there is the resurrection for "those who are Christs at His coming", who receive glorified bodies. Finally, there is the resurrection that Daniel calls "disgrace and everlasting contempt."

> "Many of those who <u>sleep in the dust of the ground will awake</u>, these to everlasting life, but

the <u>others to disgrace *and* everlasting contempt</u>. (Daniel 12:2)

"[T]hose who are Christ's at His coming" are the first resurrection, because they are given glorified bodies, and are raised before those who are raised to "disgrace and everlasting contempt." That first resurrection, when the dead in Christ rise, takes place before the rapture.

> 15 For this we say to you by the word of the Lord, that we who are alive and remain until the coming of the Lord, <u>will not precede those who have fallen asleep</u>.
> 16 For the Lord Himself will descend from heaven with a shout, with the voice of *the* archangel and with the trumpet of God, and <u>the dead in Christ will rise first</u>.
> 17 <u>Then we who are alive and remain will be caught up</u> together with them in the clouds to meet the Lord in the air, and so we shall always be with the Lord. (1 Thessalonians 4:15-17)

The rapture will take place before the wrath of God (1 Thessalonians 5:9)

Each of the four rapture views place the rapture before the wrath of God. As Pre-Wrath author Marvin Rosenthal pointed out:

> "Interestingly enough, pretribulationism, midtribulationism, and Gundry's posttribulationism would claim they are pre-

wrath too, but their identifying names do not use that designation." (Marvin Rosenthal, the Pre-Wrath Rapture of the Church, page 59)

Like Mid-Tribulationalists, Post-Tribulationalists would also limit the wrath of God to only include the seven bowls of the wrath of God.

> 1 Then I heard a loud voice from the temple, saying to the seven angels, "Go and pour out on the earth the <u>seven bowls of the wrath of God</u>." (Revelation 16:1)

Part III:
Rapture Fusion

What is Rapture Fusion?

Several years ago a gourmet food truck craze started in Southern California. One of the first was a "Korean BBQ/Taco Fusion" truck. They took the best Korean cuisine, Korean BBQ, wrapped it in the best hand-held eating device, a Mexican tortilla, and came up with something even better. *Rapture Fusion* is taking the best aspects of the four futurist Pre-Millennial rapture views to combine them into something even better.

By "best," I do not mean the main point of each view, nor an essential point of each view, nor the aspect of each view that makes one feel happiest. Rather, by "best" I mean taking the aspects of each view that do not contradict scripture, and when put together, form a cohesive structure from which to view all end times passages. Points were excluded if they did not fit with all of scripture. By "better," I mean there are flaws with each of the views, which will be further discussed in later chapters, but when the best of each view is put together, a better system can be created that fits nicely with all of scripture.

So, what can we take from each of the major rapture views to fuse into something better? I believe the best of the **Pre-Tribulation** view is the application of 1 Thessalonians 1:10 and 1 Thessalonians 5:9, that believers will not have to endure the wrath of God. The Pre-Tribulation view also gives us the nice structure of Daniel's seventieth seven (Daniel 9:27) before the coming of Christ. The **Mid-Tribulation** view has the rapture occurring at the seventh and last trumpet (1 Corinthians 15:51-52, and Revelation 11:15-17). By default, this view also suggests that the first of the seven trumpets sounds before the midpoint of the tribulation. The **Pre-Wrath** view elaborates on the Pre-Tribulational view of the rapture happening before the wrath of God, and associates the wrath of God with Revelation 6:15-17. The Pre-Wrath view also connects the sky falling during the 6th seal to the Day of the Lord, and the gathering of the elect to the sky with Jesus from the Olivet Discourse in Matthew 24:29-31. The **Post-Tribulation** view provides the single second-coming of Jesus, and only one first resurrection (Revelation 20:4-6) of the dead believers. The following table summarizes the best points of the Pre-Tribulation, Mid-Tribulation, Pre-Wrath, and Post-Trib rapture views that can be fused together to make something better:

Best Features:	View:	Scripture:
Seven year tribulation	Pre-Tribulation	Daniel 9:27
Rapture before the wrath of God	Pre-Tribulation	1 Thessalonians 1:10, 5:9
Rapture at the seventh trumpet	Mid-Tribulation	1 Corinthians 15:51-52, Revelation 11:15-17
Seven trumpets start before the middle of the tribulation	Mid-Tribulation	Revelation 8-11
6th seal celestial disturbances match Jesus' rapture prerequisites	Pre-Wrath	Revelation 6:12-14 Matthew 24:29-31
Wrath of God starts after the 6th seal is opened	Pre-Wrath	Revelation 6:15-17
Only one second-coming	Post-Tribulation	Hebrews 9:28
Only one first resurrection	Post-Tribulation	Revelation 20:4-6

Steven Covey, in his book *The Seven Habits of Highly Effective People*, explains the concept of 1 + 1 = 3. Covey's point is that one person's idea plus another person's idea does not equal two ideas. Rather, they can work together to form a third,better idea. Let's see if we can take the four rapture ideas and come up with a fifth, better idea.

What is Recapitulation?

The main tool I used to develop the idea of Rapture Fusion has the fancy name, "recapitulation." It is not as scary a word as it may sound. It does not mean, to excessively use capital letters, as my wife joked. At the root of recapitulation is the word "recap" which means to go over again. So, **recapitulation is the process of going over a subject again**. It is cycling through a time period over and over. Recapitulation is also called "progressive parallelism" in William Hendriksen's (historicist A-Millennial) book *More Than Conquerors*. The term progressive parallelism is used to describe how the various sections of Revelation run in parallel to each other with a progressive intensity. Another synonymous term used is "The Simultaneous View." In layman's terms, recapitulation is **an instant replay from a different angle**.

Sporting events on television use recapitulation frequently. An exciting or controversial play will be shown over and over again from different angles to give you multiple perspectives of what took place. Sometimes the replays are slowed down to give a different effect. Sometimes the replays start at the beginning of the play and go to the climax, while others just focus on the climax. With each replay, the commentators give different analysis. They do not say the same exact words for each replay. They give added detail and more insight from each angle, which together give the viewer a complete perspective of the exciting or controversial play. Anyone who has watched sports on television is familiar with the concept of a replay.

Imagine a caveman came to your house to watch football for the first time. In fact, this is the first time the caveman has ever seen a television. You invite the caveman in, give him a root beer, and sit down to watch the game with your friends. As the first touchdown is scored, everybody gets up and cheers. The caveman gets in on the excitement and cheers, too. Then, a replay of the touchdown is shown, and the caveman gets up and starts cheering again. Somebody asks, "Hey, Caveman! Why are you cheering again?" The caveman replies, "Because they just scored another touchdown!" You go on to explain the concept of an instant replay to the caveman, and now he has a better understanding of what is being shown on television. The book of Revelation can be seen as having a similar progression as a football game on TV, punctuated by replay after replay (recapitulation). Revelation is about revealing Jesus' return, which is described repeatedly, and from many different perspectives.

Several years ago, there was a television show called *Arrested Development*. It was about the riches-to-rags story of a dysfunctional family. The creative aspect of season four was that each episode in the season was about the same time period, and the same major events. However, each episode was from a different character's perspective. You would be shown something in one episode that seemed strange and unexplained. Then a few episodes later, that same strange and unexplained event, from the current characters perspective, would make sense. By the end of the season, all of the strange events should fit together in the viewer's mind, and they could understand the entire story line. The book of Revelation uses recapitulation in much the same way. A strange event is left unexplained in one passage. Then, a few chapters later, from a different perspective, the same event is described and makes sense. By the end of Revelation, all the strange events fit together and allow us to understand the entire story line.

Recapitulation happens elsewhere in the Bible, as well. The four Gospels are a great example. Each author tells the same story, but from a different perspective, to a different target audience, and with a different purpose. Let's take a quick look at the recapitulation of the Christmas story in the four Gospels. Matthew, who was Jewish, and writing to a Jewish audience, had the intention of showing that Jesus was the "King of the Jews." Only Matthew records the fulfillment of the Jewish prophesy (Hosea 11:1, and Matthew 2:15), that Jesus came out of Egypt, because his family fled there right before King Herod killed all the baby boys in Bethlehem. The reason King Herod knew of the newborn king was because a group of Magi came to him to find out where the new king was, so they could give Him gifts. Matthew is the only Gospel writer to record the Magi. However, Matthew omits the visit of the shepherds, presumably because shepherds are not relevant when showing that Jesus is the King of the Jews.

Mark, also Jewish but writing to Gentiles, had the likely intent of showing Jesus in action, and completely omits the Christmas story. Jesus was not in action when he was a baby, so his birth was not relevant to Mark's purpose. Others believe Mark's goal was to show Jesus as the "Suffering Servant." Do you know the birth story of your housekeeper, or gardener, or server at your local restaurant? Probably not, because it is not usually relevant to know the birth story of a servant.

On the other hand, Luke, who was a medical doctor, writing to a Gentile with the intention of giving a consecutive account (Luke 1:3) about Jesus, went into great detail on the birth of Jesus. He recorded aspects of the Christmas story others did not.

John, writing a spiritual gospel, summarized the Christmas story in only one verse, "And the Word became flesh, and dwelt among us, and we saw His glory, glory as of the only begotten from the Father, full of grace and truth." (John 1:14). Each of the Gospel writers described Jesus' first coming from different perspectives and with different purposes. Revelation is much the same way, telling the story of Jesus' second coming from multiple perspectives, and with different purposes.

We also see recapitulation in other apocalyptic literature. Daniel 2 speaks of future kingdoms (from Daniel's perspective), concluding with:

> "In the days of those kings the God of heaven will set up <u>a kingdom which will never be destroyed,</u> and that kingdom will not be left for another people; it will crush and put an end to all these kingdoms, but it will itself endure forever. (Daniel 2:44)

The kingdoms are then described again in a different way in Daniel 7. Which again concludes with God's future kingdom.

> 13 "I kept looking in the night visions,
> And behold, with the clouds of heaven

One like a Son of Man was coming,
And He came up to the Ancient of Days
And was presented before Him.
14 "And to Him was given dominion,
Glory and a kingdom,
That all the peoples, nations and *men of every*
language
Might serve Him.
His dominion is an everlasting dominion
Which will not pass away;
And His kingdom is one
Which will not be destroyed. (Daniel 7:13-14)

Daniel 8 also speaks of future kingdoms, as does Daniel 9, Daniel 10, and Daniel 11. Daniel 12 includes the resurrection:

1 "Now at that time Michael, the great prince who stands guard over the sons of your people, will arise. And there will be a time of distress such as never occurred since there was a nation until that time; and at that time your people, everyone who is found written in the book, will be rescued.
2 "Many of those who sleep in the dust of the ground will awake, these to everlasting life, but the others to disgrace and everlasting contempt.
3 "Those who have insight will shine brightly like the brightness of the expanse of heaven, and those who lead the many to righteousness, like the stars forever and ever. (Daniel 12:1-3)

Since the book of Daniel is of the same genre as Revelation, and Daniel obviously uses recapitulation, it should be easy to understand that John uses recapitulation as well.

Where is Recapitulation in Revelation?

Many people in the church have read Revelation and finish feeling dazed and confused. I think there are several reasons for this. First, we should be asking the Holy Spirit, through prayer, to give us ears to hear what He said to the churches. Eight times in Revelation is a similar phrase, "If anyone has an ear, let him hear." (Revelation 13:9). That statement implies, some in the church are not given an ear to hear. Have you asked for an ear to hear today? If not, take a moment in prayer and ask the Holy Spirit to give you ears to hear.

> 27 As for you, <u>the anointing</u> which you received from Him <u>abides in you</u>, and you have no need for anyone to teach you; but as <u>His anointing teaches you</u> about all things, and is true and is not a lie, and just as it has taught you, you abide in Him.
>
> 28 Now, little children, <u>abide in Him</u>, so that <u>when He appears, we may have confidence and not</u>

shrink away from Him in shame at His coming. (1
John 2:27-28)

The second reason I think people are so confused after reading
Revelation is because they do not know the Old Testament well
enough. Revelation has hundreds of references to the Old
Testament, and we need to be more familiar with them. A
practical application one could derive from reading Revelation
is the encouragement to study the Old Testament. Finally, I
think one of the main reasons why people struggle with
Revelation is because they assume it is chronological. This is a
logical assumption to start with, but once we see that it is not
chronological, we need to start figuring out the structure. That
is where recapitulation comes in.

It would be an oversimplification of Revelation's recapitulation
to say the first seal is the same event as the first trumpet and the
same event as the first bowl. That would be like saying the
Magi in Matthew's Christmas story are the shepherds of Luke's
Christmas story. While both Matthew and Luke are describing
the events around the birth of Jesus, they each include and
exclude different parts of the Christmas story in order to make
their points to their audience. While portions of Revelation
cover similar periods of time, there is not always a one-to-one
correspondence in each parallel description of the end times.

It is very easy to prove Revelation is not chronological. I will
start with the most clear example, then go through each cycle
one-by-one. At the seventh trumpet, John writes:

> 15 Then the seventh angel sounded; and there
> were loud voices in heaven, saying, "The kingdom
> of the world has become the kingdom of our Lord
> and of His Christ; and He will reign forever and

ever."

16 And the twenty-four elders, who sit on their thrones before God, fell on their faces and worshiped God,

17 saying, "We give You thanks, O Lord God, the Almighty, who are and who were, because You have taken Your great power and have begun to reign. (Revelation 11:15-17)

At the seventh trumpet, the kingdom comes, "The kingdom of the world has become the kingdom of our Lord and of His Christ" (Revelation 11:15). This is the answer to nearly 2,000 years of prayer, "Your kingdom come. Your will be done on earth as it is in heaven" (Matthew 6:10).

The kingdom coming is followed by wrath, judgment, rewards, and acts of God.

18 "And the nations were enraged, and Your wrath came, and the time came for the dead to be judged, and the time to reward Your bond-servants the prophets and the saints and those who fear Your name, the small and the great, and to destroy those who destroy the earth."

19 And the temple of God which is in heaven was opened; and the ark of His covenant appeared in His temple, and there were flashes of lightning and sounds and peals of thunder and an earthquake and a great hailstorm. (Revelation 11:18-19)

Revelation 11 brings us to the end of the end times, when the kingdom comes in full force. Then, in chapter 12 of Revelation, we are taken back to the first century, when Jesus is born. John starts the end times story over again, by taking us back to the birth of Jesus, just so we cannot miss that he is starting over again.

> 5 And she gave birth to a son, a male *child*, who is to rule all the nations with a rod of iron; and her child was caught up to God and to His throne. (Revelation 12:5)

Jesus is born in His first coming, in Revelation 12:5. However, by the time we get to the very next verse, we are in the last three-and-a-half-years of the tribulation again, for the retelling of Daniel's 70th seven, from a different perspective.

> 6 Then the woman fled into the wilderness where she had a place prepared by God, so that there she would be nourished for one thousand two hundred and sixty days. (Revelation 12:6)

The 1,260 days are 3.5 years, the last half of Daniel's seventieth seven. The same amount of time the two witnesses of Revelation 11 prophesy:

> "And I will grant *authority* to my two witnesses, and they will prophesy for twelve hundred and sixty days, clothed in sackcloth." (Revelation 11:3)

The recapitulation between Revelation 11:14-19 and Revelation 12:1-6 should be very clear. In Revelation 11:15-19 the kingdom comes as we conclude the tribulation, then Revelation 12:1-6 starts over with the birth of Christ and concludes with the last 1,260 days of tribulation.

Below is an outline of the book of Revelation, based on recapitulation:

I. **The Things Which You Have Seen** (Revelation 1)
   A. Introduction (Revelation 1:1-8)
   B. Vision of Jesus, 7 lamp-stands, 7 stars (Revelation 1:9-20)
II. **The Things Which Are** (Revelation 2-3)
   A. Message to Ephesus (Revelation 2:1-7)
   B. Message to Smyrna (Revelation 2:8-11)
   C. Message to Pergamum (Revelation 2:12-17)
   D. Message to Thyatira (Revelation 2:18-29)
   E. Message to Sardis (Revelation 3:1-6)
   F. Message to Philadelphia (Revelation 3:7-13)
   G. Message to Laodicea (Revelation 3:14-22)
III. **The Things Which Will Take Place After These Things** (Revelation 4-22)
   A. 6 Seals with an Earthquake (Revelation 4-6)
   B. 144,000, Great Multitude, 7th Seal (Revelation 7-8:1)
   C. 6 Trumpets, Strong Messenger, 7 Thunders, Little Scroll (Revelation 8:2-10:11)
   D. 2 Witnesses with an Earthquake (Revelation 11:1-11:13)
   E. 7th Trumpet (Kingdom of our Lord), Lightning, Thunder, Earthquake, and Hail (Revelation 11:14-11:19)
   F. Birth of Jesus, Dragon, Woman in the Wilderness (Revelation 12:1-6)
   G. Dragon, Woman in the Wilderness, War with Jesus Witnesses (Revelation 12:7-17)
   H. Beast from the Sea, Beast From the Earth, Lamb on Mt. Zion (Revelation 13:1-14:5)
   I. 3 Angels' Announcements, 2 Reapings (Revelation 14:6-20)
   J. 7 Bowls of the Wrath of God; Lightning, Thunder, Earthquake, and Hail (Revelation 15-16)

K. Babylon, Thunder, Coming of the King, 1,000 Years (Revelation 17:1-20:3)

L. 1,000 Years, Great White Throne, New: Heaven, Earth, Jerusalem (Revelation 20:4-22:21)

John and Jesus give us the start of our outline in Revelation 1:19.

> 19 "Therefore write <u>the things which you have seen,</u> and <u>the things which are,</u> and <u>the things which will take place after these things.</u> (Revelation 1:19)

Revelation 1 contains "things which you have seen," namely the vision of Jesus with the seven stars and seven lamp stands. Revelation 2-3 are "the things which are", seven letters to specific churches in the first century. Those churches would be in modern-day Turkey. Revelation 4-22 are "the things that will take place after these things" or future events.

Roman numeral III of our outline, "The Things Which Will Take Place After These Things," shows how John tells us the same story 12 times, each time with a different purpose. The majority of Pre-Millennialists, regardless of their rapture position, would probably place the end times events in the following chronological order:

1. Resurrection
2. Rapture
3. Wrath of God
4. Armageddon Starts
5. Second Coming
6. Armageddon Ends
7. 1,000 Year Reign

In each of the outlined sections A-L, various events from this list of seven, and others, are described. Each lettered section is a different cycle, a parallel account, and a recapitulation of the end times events.

Now that we understand the most obvious recapitulation between Revelation 11:14-19 and Revelation 12:1-6, and have an outline for Revelation, let's now look at each of the recapitulations in the category of "things to come".

A. 6 Seals with an Earthquake (Revelation 4-6)

Revelation 4-6 is about the seals. Chapter 5, an introduction to the seals, features the slain Lamb taking the scroll with seven seals from Him who sat on the throne. Chapter 4 is an introduction to the introduction in Chapter 5, describing Him who sat on the throne. Chapter 6 is about the breaking of six of the seals on the scroll. After each of the first four seals is broken, one of the four horsemen of the apocalypse is released. The fifth seal is a heavenly scene of the martyrs under the altar asking:

> "How long, O Lord, holy and true, will You refrain from judging and avenging our blood on those who dwell on the earth?"
> 11 And there was given to each of them a white robe; and they were told that they should rest for a little while longer, until the number of their fellow servants and their brethren who were to be killed even as they had been, would be completed also. (Revelation 6:10b-11)

The sixth seal is quite interesting. This seal is the main support for the Pre-Wrath rapture view.

12 I looked when He broke the sixth seal, and there was a great earthquake; and the sun became black as sackcloth *made* of hair, and the whole moon became like blood;

13 and the stars of the sky fell to the earth, as a fig tree casts its unripe figs when shaken by a great wind.

14 The sky was split apart like a scroll when it is rolled up, and every mountain and island were moved out of their places.

15 Then the kings of the earth and the great men and the commanders and the rich and the strong and every slave and free man hid themselves in the caves and among the rocks of the mountains;

16 and they said to the mountains and to the rocks, "Fall on us and hide us from the presence of Him who sits on the throne, and from the wrath of the Lamb;

17 for the great day of their wrath has come, and who is able to stand?" (Revelation 6:12-17)

While I am not going to go into all the details of this passage, I will try to highlight the main points that pertain to the Pre-Wrath view. The effects of each of the broken seals described in Revelation 6 closely match the order of the end time events Jesus describes in Matthew 24. The "Harmony of the gospel writers at a glance" table on page 56 lists the passages that correspond. Here, I will only point out the similarities between the sixth seal and portions of the Olivet Discourse:

15 "Therefore when you see the abomination of desolation which was spoken of through Daniel

the prophet, standing in the holy place (let the reader understand) (Matthew 24:15)

29 "But <u>immediately after the tribulation</u> of those days THE SUN WILL BE DARKENED, AND THE MOON WILL NOT GIVE ITS LIGHT, AND THE STARS WILL FALL <u>from the sky</u>, and the powers of the heavens will be shaken. 30 "And then <u>the sign of the Son of Man will appear in the sky</u>, and then all the tribes of the earth will mourn, and <u>they will see the SON OF MAN COMING ON THE CLOUDS OF THE SKY</u> with power and great glory.
31 "And He will send forth His angels with A GREAT <u>TRUMPET</u> and <u>THEY WILL GATHER TOGETHER His elect from the four winds, from one end of the sky to the other.</u> (Matthew 24:29-31)

Note that the abomination of desolation in Matthew 24:15 is the midpoint of Daniel's 70th seven, the tribulation, and is mentioned several verses before the effects of the 6th seal in Matthew 24:29. This places the 6th seal after the abomination of desolation. More specifically, Matthew 24:29-31 and the sixth seal are "immediately after the tribulation". Both Matthew 24:29-31 and Revelation 6:12-17 describe the sun, moon, stars, and sky in a similar fashion. Both passages have people on earth viewing Jesus (AKA the Lamb, and the Son of Man) in the sky. Matthew 24:31 says the angels "WILL GATHER TOGETHER His elect from the four winds, from one end of the sky to the other." Matthew 24:31 is a rapture passage. The elect are gathered to the sky. It also includes a trumpet, as do other resurrection/rapture passages, such as 1 Thessalonians 4:16-17 and 1 Corinthians 15:51-52.

16 For the Lord Himself will descend from heaven with a shout, with the voice of *the* archangel and with the <u>trumpet of God</u>, and the <u>dead</u> in Christ <u>will rise</u> first.

17 Then we who are alive and remain will be <u>caught up</u> together with them <u>in the clouds to meet the Lord in the air</u>, and so we shall always be with the Lord. (1 Thessalonians 4:16-17)

51 Behold, I tell you a mystery; we will not all sleep, but we will all be changed,

52 in a moment, in the twinkling of an eye, <u>at the last trumpet; for the trumpet will sound, and the dead will be raised imperishable, and we will be changed</u>. (1 Corinthians 15:51-52)

Revelation 6:15-17 says those on the earth will say the "wrath has come", after they see Jesus in the sky. This is the first use of the word "wrath" in Revelation. It would not be logical to retroactively apply the wrath of God to anything prior to Revelation 6:15. Bad things happen as the Lamb removes the seals of protection, but those bad things are not the wrath of God. 1 Thessalonians 1:10 and 1 Thessalonians 5:9 inform us that believers will not have to endure the wrath of God.

10 and to wait for His Son from heaven, whom He raised from the dead, *that is* Jesus, who rescues us from the wrath to come. (1 Thessalonians 1:10)

9 For God has not destined us for wrath, but for obtaining salvation through our Lord Jesus Christ, (1 Thessalonians 5:9)

Therefore, it can be inferred that the rapture takes place at Revelation 6:14, after the sky splits, and before the wrath of the Lamb in Revelation 6:15-17. This is the main point of the Pre-Wrath view. The "wrath" brings us to the end of the age, to the end of this section of Revelation, and to the end of this section of the outline. We have just completed our first pass through Daniel's 70th seven. From the outline, III.A. 6 Seals with an Earthquake (Revelation 4-6), could be summarized as, "**Inferred Resurrection and Rapture before the Wrath of God**".

I.   The things which you have seen (Revelation 1)
II. The things which are (Revelation 2-3)
III. The things which will take place after these things (Revelation 4-22)
    A. Inferred Resurrection and Rapture before the Wrath of God (Revelation 4-6)

B. 144,000, Great Multitude, 7th Seal (Revelation 7-8:1)

Now that we have made our first pass through the end times, we start over again. Revelation 7 is an interlude that falls between the 6th and 7th seals in John's writing, but does not fall between the 6th and 7th seals chronologically. John formed a pattern while writing about the seals, trumpets, and bowls. He wrote about the first 6, inserted an interlude, and then finished with the seventh. His first interlude, Revelation 7:1-8, is about the sealing of the 144,000 sons of Israel.

> 3 saying, "<u>Do not harm</u> the earth or the sea or the trees <u>until</u> we have <u>sealed the bond-servants</u> of our God on their foreheads."
> 4 And I heard the number of those who were sealed, <u>one hundred and forty-four thousand</u>

sealed from every tribe of the sons of Israel:
(Revelation 7:3-4)

John places this interlude here to contrast the removal of the
protective seals of the scroll and the bad things that happen as a
result, with the application of seals to the bond-servants and the
protection that results. Notice this sealing happens before the
earth, sea, and trees are harmed. This likely means the seals
needed to be placed before the "four horsemen of the
apocalypse" brought famine and pestilence on the earth.

> Authority was given to them over a fourth of the
> earth, to kill with sword and with famine and
> with pestilence and by the wild beasts of the
> earth. (Revelation 6:8b)

It would not make sense to place this seal of protection on the
144,000 after "the great day of their wrath has come"
(Revelation 6:17b). This also implies the sealing of the 144,000 is
not chronologically after the 6th seal.

After 144,000 of the sons of Israel are sealed, we are told of a
second group, "a great multitude from every nation."

> 9 After these things I looked, and behold, a great
> multitude which no one could count, from every
> nation and all tribes and peoples and tongues,
> standing before the throne and before the Lamb,
> clothed in white robes, and palm branches were in
> their hands; (Revelation 7:9)

This "great multitude" standing before the throne in white
robes, should remind us of the martyrs under the altar at the 5th
seal, who were given white robes.

9 When the Lamb broke the fifth seal, I saw underneath the altar the souls of those who had been slain because of the word of God, and because of the testimony which they had maintained; (Revelation 6:9)

11 And there was given to each of them a white robe; and they were told that they should rest for a little while longer, until *the number of* their fellow servants and their brethren who were to be killed even as they had been, would be completed also. (Revelation 6:11)

By Revelation 7:9, those given white robes under the altar are now standing before the throne and Lamb. The martyred souls seem to have been resurrected. 1 Thessalonians 4:16 informs us that the dead rise first.

16 For the Lord Himself will descend from heaven with a shout, with the voice of *the* archangel and with the trumpet of God, and the dead in Christ will rise first. (1 Thessalonians 4:16)

Revelation 8:1 brings us to another conclusion of the tribulation, Daniel's 70th seven. After the 144,000 are sealed, and those given white robes are standing before the throne and Lamb, the 7th seal is broken.

1 When the Lamb broke the seventh seal, there was silence in heaven for about half an hour. (Revelation 8:1)

We are not told any more details about the silence in Revelation 8, so we need to look elsewhere to find out more about this

silence. Notice that the silence is in heaven. Throughout
Revelation, John describes all the various sounds he hears in
heaven. For example:

> 8 And the four living creatures, each one of them
> having six wings, are full of eyes around and
> within; and <u>day and night they do not cease to
> say,</u>
> "HOLY, HOLY, HOLY *is* THE LORD GOD, THE ALMIGHTY,
> WHO WAS AND WHO IS AND WHO IS TO COME."
> (Revelation 4:8)

However, Revelation 8:1 is different. There is silence in heaven.
Take a look at what is said before the bowls of the wrath of God
are poured out.

> 7 Then one of the four living creatures gave to the
> seven angels seven golden <u>bowls full of the wrath
> of God,</u> who lives forever and ever.
> 8 And the <u>temple</u> was filled with smoke from the
> glory of <u>God</u> and from His power; and <u>no one was
> able to enter the temple until the seven plagues of
> the seven angels were finished.</u> (Revelation 15:7-8)

While the wrath of God is poured out, the temple in heaven is
closed off. This causes a temporary pause in the worship of
God, resulting in silence. Let's see if that fits with passages
outside of Revelation.

> **7** <u>Be silent before the Lord GOD!</u>
> For the <u>day of the LORD</u> is near,
> For the LORD has prepared a sacrifice,
> He has consecrated His guests. (Zephaniah 1:7)

94

14 Near is the great day of the LORD,
Near and coming very quickly;
Listen, the day of the LORD!
In it the warrior cries out bitterly.
15 A day of wrath is that day,
A day of trouble and distress,
A day of destruction and desolation,
A day of darkness and gloom,
A day of clouds and thick darkness,
16 A day of trumpet and battle cry
Against the fortified cities
And the high corner towers. (Zephaniah 1:14-16)

Zephaniah 1:7, 14-16, describes a silence before the Lord during the day of the Lord, while on Earth there is wrath, darkness, clouds, and a trumpet. It would appear that the 7th seal is the silence after the sun and moon go dark, after the rapture trumpet, and during the wrath of God. Zechariah gives a similar account of the silence.

10 "Sing for joy and be glad, O daughter of Zion; for behold I am coming and I will dwell in your midst," declares the Lord.
11 "Many nations will join themselves to the Lord in that day and will become My people. Then I will dwell in your midst, and you will know that the Lord of hosts has sent Me to you.
12 "The Lord will possess Judah as His portion in the holy land, and will again choose Jerusalem.
13 "Be silent, all flesh, before the Lord; for He is aroused from His holy habitation." (Zechariah 2:10-13)

Zechariah writes of the silence before the Second Coming, which is after the wrath. Therefore Revelation 15:7-8, Zephaniah 1:14-16, and Zechariah 2:10-13 all point to the silence of the 7th seal being during the wrath of God.

From our second pass through the end times from Revelation 7:1-8:1, we see seals of protection, the resurrection, and we can infer the wrath of God. As seven is a symbol of completion, the seventh seal completes the end of the age. This section of Revelation was our second cycle, parallel account, or recapitulation. We could update this section of the Revelation outline for III.B. to **Resurrection, and Inferred Wrath of God**. When we compare this summary with that from III.A., "Inferred Resurrection and Rapture before the Wrath of God", we can see that Revelation 4-6 and Revelation 7:1-8:1 are roughly in parallel, covering a similar period of time and similar events, but from a different perspective.

I.   The things which you have seen (Revelation 1)
II. The things which are (Revelation 2-3)
III. The things which will take place after these things (Revelation 4-22)
   A. Inferred Resurrection and Rapture before the Wrath of God (Revelation 4-6)
   B. Resurrection, and Inferred Wrath of God (Revelation 7-8:1)

C. 6 Trumpets, Strong Messenger, 7 Thunders, Little Scroll (Revelation 8:2-10:11)

Revelation 8:2 begins the section with a common phrase in Revelation, "And I saw" or "Then I saw." The phrase does not necessarily convey the order the events will occur, but rather, the order John saw the scenes. It would be similar to saying, "I saw a World War II documentary, then I saw a World War I documentary." That does not mean the second war came before the first, it only conveys the order in which I saw the documentaries. Likewise, this section on the trumpets probably starts before the seals, but John saw the vision of the trumpets after the vision of the seals.

In the third recapitulation, we hear the trumpets. The trumpets are warnings.

> 2 "Son of man, speak to the sons of your people and say to them, 'If I bring a sword upon a land, and the people of the land take one man from among them and make him their <u>watchman</u>, 3 and he sees the sword coming upon the land and blows on the <u>trumpet</u> and <u>warns the people</u>, 4 then he who hears the sound of the <u>trumpet</u> and does not take <u>warning</u>, and a sword comes and takes him away, his blood will be on his *own* head. 5 'He heard the sound of the <u>trumpet</u> but did not take <u>warning</u>; his blood will be on himself. But had he taken <u>warning</u>, he would have delivered his life.
> 6 'But if the <u>watchman</u> sees the sword coming and does not blow the <u>trumpet</u> and the people are not <u>warned</u>, and a sword comes and takes a person from them, he is taken away in his iniquity; but his blood I will require from the <u>watchman's</u> hand.' (Ezekiel 33:2-6)

The watchmen are to look for the sign, then blow the trumpets to warn the people of what is coming. Revelation 8:2-6 is an introduction to the seven trumpets, as Revelation 4-5 is an introduction to the seven seals.

Revelation 8:2-6 has a Chiastic Structure. These structures were often used in ancient writings as a method to make a point. The first and last parts go together, and the second and second to last parts go together, and so on. The middle of the structure is the emphasis of the passage.

> 2 And I saw the seven angels who stand before God, and seven trumpets were given to them.
> 3 Another angel came and stood at the altar, holding a golden censer; and much incense was given to him, so that he might add it to the prayers of all the saints on the golden altar which was before the throne.
> 4 And the smoke of the incense, with the prayers of the saints, went up before God out of the angel's hand.
> 5 Then the angel took the censer and filled it with the fire of the altar, and threw it to the earth; and there followed peals of thunder and sounds and flashes of lightning and an earthquake.
> 6 And the seven angels who had the seven trumpets prepared themselves to sound them.
> (Revelation 8:2-6)

A. Seven angels given seven trumpets (Revelation 8:2)
 B. Alter (Revelation 8:3)
  C. Censer (Revelation 8:3)
   D. Prayers (Revelation 8:3)
    E. Golden altar before the throne (Revelation 8:3)
   D' Prayers (Revelation 8:4)
  C' Censer (Revelation 8:5)
 B' Alter (Revelation 8:5)
A' Seven angels given seven trumpets (Revelation 8:6)

In fact, all of Revelation has a Chiastic Structure, emphasizing Jesus kingdom taking over Satan's kingdom.

A. Introduction (Revelation 1)
  B. Believers on the Earth (Revelation 2-3)
   C. The Throne (Revelation 4)
    D. Lamb Slain (Revelation 6)
     E. Seven Seals (Revelation 6:1-8:1)
      F. Six Angels Trumpets (Revelation 8:2-9:21)
       G. Strong Messenger (Revelation 10)
        H. Two Witnesses (Revelation 11:1-13)
        I. Jesus (Revelation 11:14-19)
        I' Satan (Revelation 12)
        H' Two Beasts (Revelation 13)
       G' Triumphant Lamb (Revelation 14:1-5)
      F' Six Angels Announcements (Revelation 14:6-20)
     E' Seven Bowls (Revelation 15-16)
    D' Jesus Slaying (Revelation 19)
   C' The Thrones (Revelation 20)
  B' Believers on the New Earth (Revelation 21:1-22:5)
A' Conclusion (Revelation 22:6-21)

If you take a look at the Table of Contents, you may notice *Rapture Fusion* is written in a Chiastic structure as well.

The first trumpet warns of the "four angels standing at the four corners of the earth" (Revelation 7:1), who were commanded "Do not harm the earth or the sea or the trees until we have sealed the bond-servants of our God on their foreheads." (Revelation 7:3). For they are now allowed to harm the earth, sea, and trees.

> **7** The <u>first sounded</u>, and there came hail and fire, mixed with blood, and they were thrown to the earth; and a third of the <u>earth</u> was burned up, and

a third of the <u>trees</u> were burned up, and all the green grass was burned up. (Revelation 8:7)

8 The <u>second angel sounded</u>, and *something* <u>like</u> a <u>great mountain</u> <u>burning</u> with fire was <u>thrown</u> into the <u>sea</u>; and a third of the sea became blood, (Revelation 8:8)

The second trumpet also provides a warning. This time the warning is for "something like a great burning mountain". Note it is not a mountain, but something else. 1 Enoch is not scripture, but it was known to the first century church, we know this because Jude quoted from it. So the first century church was aware of the symbols in 1 Enoch, which included burning mountains.

14 And there I beheld seven <u>stars</u>, like <u>great</u> <u>blazing mountains</u>, and like spirits entreating me. 15 Then the angel said, This place, until the consummation of heaven and earth, will be the <u>prison of the stars</u>, and the host of heaven. 16 <u>The stars</u> which roll over fire <u>are those which</u> <u>transgressed the commandment of God</u> before their time arrived; for they came not in their proper season. Therefore was He offended with them, and bound them, until the period of the consummation of their crimes in the secret year. (1 Enoch 18:14-16)

3 There, too, I beheld seven <u>stars</u> of heaven <u>bound</u> in it together, like <u>great mountains, and like a</u> <u>blazing fire</u>. I exclaimed, For what species of <u>crime</u> have they been bound, and why have they been

removed to this place? Then Uriel, one of the holy angels who was with me, and who conducted me, answered: Enoch, wherefore do you ask; wherefore do you reason with yourself, and anxiously inquire? These are those of the <u>stars which have transgressed the commandment of the most high God</u>; and are here bound, until the infinite number of the days of their crimes be completed. (1 Enoch 21:3)

From the two passages in 1 Enoch, we know that burning mountains symbolized fallen angels. Another clue in Revelation 8:8 is that the great burning mountain was thrown. It happens that there is a fallen angel who is thrown in Revelation.

9 And <u>the great dragon was thrown down,</u> the serpent of old who is <u>called the devil and Satan,</u> who deceives the whole world; <u>he was thrown down to the earth,</u> and his angels were thrown down with him. (Revelation 12:9)

The second trumpet warns that the fallen angel, Satan, is coming. Ian Boxall wrote in *Black's New Testament Commentary: The Revelation of Saint John*:

More likely, we are to think of the mountain-like object as a fallen angel, as are the seven stars 'like great burning mountains' that Enoch witnesses at the end of heaven and earth (1 En. 18:13–14; 21:3; cf. 108:4; the similarity of John's description to a meteorite has been noted by Roloff 1993: 110). The verb used of this fallen star/angel (was thrown) places it in the same league as Satan, the monster, and the false prophet (12:9, 10, 13; 19:20; 20:10, 14, 15). (Boxall 2006: Revelation 8:8–9)

The third trumpet:

> 10 The <u>third angel sounded</u>, and a great <u>star fell from heaven</u>, burning like a torch, and it fell on a third of the rivers and on the springs of waters. 11 The name of the star is called <u>Wormwood</u>; and a third of the waters became wormwood, and many men died from the waters, because they were made bitter. (Revelation 8:10-11)

Wormwood is obviously not a literal star. A literal star falling to earth would affect much more than a third of the fresh water, so it is obviously symbolic. Furthermore, the fallen "star" is able to use a key, and open the abyss (Revelation 9:1). Wormwood is a demon that most likely empowers the false prophet, described in Revelation 13:11-18, 16:13-16, and 19:20.

> 12 The <u>fourth angel sounded</u>, and a third of the sun and a third of the moon and <u>a third of the stars were struck</u>, so that a third of them would be darkened and the day would not shine for a third of it, and the night in the same way. (Revelation 8:12)

A "third of the stars were struck" (Revelation 9:12) is very similar to "And his tail swept away a third of the stars of heaven and threw them to the earth." (Revelation 12:4) "and his angels were thrown down with him" (Revelation 12:9). So the fourth trumpet warns of Satan's fallen angels.

1 Then the <u>fifth angel sounded</u>, and I saw a <u>star from heaven which had fallen to the earth</u>; and the <u>key</u> of the <u>bottomless pit</u> was given to him.
2 He <u>opened the bottomless pit</u>, and smoke went up out of the pit, like the smoke of a great furnace; and the sun and the air were darkened by the smoke of the pit. (Revelation 9:1-2)

11 They have as king over them, <u>the angel of the abyss</u>; his name in Hebrew is <u>Abaddon</u>, and in the Greek he has the name <u>Apollyon</u>. (Revelation 9:11)

The "star" in Revelation 9:1 is Wormwood, whom we met at the third trumpet. He opens the abyss for Apollyon or Abaddon, both names meaning destroyer. Apollyon is the king of the abyss, and the demons (locust) found there. The beast from the abyss is described elsewhere in Revelation, "the beast that comes up out of the abyss will make war with them [the two witnesses], and overcome them and kill them [the two witnesses]." (Revelation 11:7b), Revelation 13:1-10, "The beast that you saw was, and is not, and is about to come up out of the abyss and go to destruction." (Revelation 17:8a), and Revelation 19:20. The beast from the abyss is commonly known as the Antichrist. The name "Antichrist" is never used in the book of Revelation. Ironically, the term "antichrist" is used exclusively in John's other epistles (e.g. 1 John 2:18). The person often called the Antichrist, is called the little horn in Daniel 7:8, 24-27, the prince or ruler in Daniel 9:26-27, the king in Daniel 11:36-12:13, the man of lawlessness and the son of destruction (apolia) in 2 Thessalonians 2:1-4. So the 5th trumpet warns of the Antichrist.

So far, the **first trumpet warned of four destructive angels**, the **second trumpet warned of Satan**, the **third trumpet warned of the false prophet**, the **fourth trumpet warned of the fallen**

angels, and the **fifth trumpet warned of the Antichrist**. Satan, the false prophet, and the Antichrist all need to be on the scene by the abomination of desolation, or 3.5 years into the tribulation. Since the sixth seal had to have been opened after the abomination of desolation, and the first five trumpets had to have been opened before the abomination of desolation, the opening of the first five seals and the blowing of the first five trumpets must be in parallel. Recapitulation must be taking place, as we are now into our third telling of the story, first with the six seals, then with the 144,000 great multitude, and the seventh seal, and finally with the trumpets.

> 13 Then the <u>sixth angel sounded,</u> and I heard a voice from the four horns of the golden altar which is before God,
> 14 one saying to the sixth angel who had the trumpet, <u>"Release the four angels who are bound at the great river Euphrates."</u> (Revelation 9:13-14)

The **sixth trumpet warns of four bound angels**. Since they are bound they must be fallen angels, or demons. The four bound angels bring forth the armies of two hundred million, in Revelation 9:16. This is the start of Armageddon, near the end of Daniel's 70th seven, and well after the Abomination of Desolation.

After the first six seals is another interlude for chapter 10 and half of chapter 11. The first part of the interlude continues from where the sixth trumpet left off.

> 1 I saw another <u>strong angel</u> <u>coming down out of heaven,</u> clothed with a <u>cloud;</u> and the <u>rainbow</u> was upon his head, and his <u>face was like the sun,</u> and his <u>feet like pillars of fire;</u>

2 and he had in his hand a little book which was
open. He placed his right foot on the sea and his
left on the land;
3 and he cried out with a loud voice, as when a
lion roars; and when he had cried out, the seven
peals of thunder uttered their voices. (Revelation
10:1-3)

Compare with the following verses:

7 BEHOLD, HE IS COMING WITH THE CLOUDS, and
every eye will see Him, even those who pierced
Him; and all the tribes of the earth will mourn
over Him. So it is to be. Amen.(Revelation 1:7)

15 His feet *were* like burnished bronze, when it has
been made to glow in a furnace, and His voice *was*
like the sound of many waters.
16 In His right hand He held seven stars, and out
of His mouth came a sharp two-edged sword; and
His face was like the sun shining in its strength.
(Revelation 1:15-16)

If the Greek word "aggelos", translated as angel in Revelation
10:1, was not used, practically everybody would agree that
Revelation 10:1-3 is a description of Jesus. So either "aggelos"
means angel, and the angel happens to look and sound a lot like
Jesus, or, the other translation of "aggelos" should be used here,
which means messenger. Then Jesus is being a messenger,
delivering the little scroll (Revelation 10:8-11). So, after the start
of Armageddon in Revelation 9:13-21, we have Jesus "right foot
on the sea and his left on the land" (Revelation 10:2). Revelation

10 is a Second Coming passage, and ends this section in the outline.

Revelation 10:3-4 also mentions, the often overlooked, seven peals of thunder. When we speak of the seven seals, the seven trumpets, and seven bowls of Revelation, we should also mention the seven thunders. It seems that the seven thunders are alluded to in upcoming recapitulations in Revelation 11:19, and Revelation 16:18.

The recapitulation in Revelation 8:2-10:11 includes the start of Armageddon, and the Second Coming of Jesus. From the outline III (C) can be summarized as **Armageddon Starts, and the Second Coming.**

I.   The things which you have seen (Revelation 1)
II. The things which are (Revelation 2-3)
III. The things which will take place after these things (Revelation 4-22)
    A. Inferred Resurrection and Rapture before the Wrath of God (Revelation 4-6)
    B. Resurrection, and Inferred Wrath of God (Revelation 7-8:1)
    C. Armageddon Starts, and the Second Coming (Revelation 8:2-10:11)

D. 2 Witnesses with an Earthquake (Revelation 11:1-11:13)

In Revelation 11:1-13, we are told about the two witnesses who prophesied for 3.5 years. Zechariah 4 describes two olive trees; one represented the builder who started and finished building the temple after the return from exile, and the other olive tree represented the high priest of the temple being rebuilt in the Old Testament. Revelation 11:4 follows the measuring of a temple, an altar, and describes the two witnesses as the two olive trees.

> 4 These are the two olive trees and the two lampstands that stand before the Lord of the earth. (Revelation 11:4)

I believe the two witnesses in Revelation 11:4 will be the future re-builder of the temple and the future high priest, just as the two Olive Trees in Zechariah 4 were the re-builder of the temple and the high priest of the newly rebuilt temple. We are told in Revelation 11:7 the two witnesses will be killed by the beast from the abyss, or the Antichrist. After 3.5 days the two witnesses are resurrected and raptured. Then there is an earthquake, similar to the earthquake found in Revelation 11:19 and Revelation 16:18, after the wrath of God is poured out. Take a look at the first ending of Revelation 11.

> 11 But after the three and a half days, the breath of life from God came into them, and they stood on their feet; and great fear fell upon those who were watching them.
> 12 And they heard a loud voice from heaven saying to them, "Come up here." Then they went up into heaven in the cloud, and their enemies watched them.
> 13 And in that hour there was a great earthquake, and a tenth of the city fell; seven thousand people were killed in the earthquake, and the rest were terrified and gave glory to the God of heaven. (Revelation 11:11-13)

Revelation 11:1-13 is our 4th recapitulation in revelation. After the 144,000 are sealed, the two witnesses prophesying overlap with the same time period as the removal of the 6th seal, and sounding of the sixth trumpet. Outline III.D. can be summarized with the **Resurrection, Rapture, and Inferred Wrath of God.**

I. The things which you have seen (Revelation 1)
II. The things which are (Revelation 2-3)
III. The things which will take place after these things (Revelation 4-22)
    A. Inferred Resurrection and Rapture before the Wrath of God (Revelation 4-6)
    B. Resurrection, and Inferred Wrath of God (Revelation 7-8:1)
    C. Armageddon Starts, and the Second Coming (Revelation 8:2-10:11)
    D. Resurrection, Rapture, and Inferred Wrath of God (Revelation 11:1-11:13)

E. 7th Trumpet (Kingdom of our Lord), Lightning, Thunder, Earthquake, and Hail (Revelation 11:14-11:19)

I have already covered this fifth section of recapitulation as the most obvious example of recapitulation, so I will not spend too much time on it. However, I cannot stress its importance enough. I believe it is the climax of Revelation, and possibly of the entire Bible. This is when the awaited kingdom comes! The kingdom has already started at Jesus' first coming (e.g. Luke 17:21), but has not yet fully come. At the seventh trumpet, "The kingdom of the world has become the kingdom of our Lord and of His Christ". The worship in Heaven changes from "who is and who was and who is to come" (Revelation 1:4, Revelation 1:8, and Revelation 4:8) to, "who are and who were." The last phrase, "and who is to come" is no longer needed, because at the seventh trumpet He just came. The first six trumpets warned of four destructive angels, Satan, the false prophet, the fallen angels, the Antichrist, and the four bound angels. The seventh trumpet announces that Jesus is back.

The phrase, "day of the Lord," is used throughout scripture.

> 30 "I will display wonders in the <u>sky</u> and on the <u>earth</u>,
> <u>Blood</u>, <u>fire</u> and columns of smoke.
> 31 "The <u>sun</u> will be turned into darkness
> And the <u>moon into blood</u>
> Before the great and awesome <u>day of the Lord</u> comes.
> 32 "And it will come about that <u>whoever calls on the name of the Lord Will be delivered</u>; (Joel 2:30-32a)

In Joel 2, the day of the Lord is described as "great and awesome", while in Malachi 4:5b, it is called "the great and terrible day of the Lord." It will bring wrath and judgment (Revelation 11:18). The wrath mentioned in Revelation 11:18 is recapitulated in Revelation 15-16, and the judgment from Revelation 11:18, is recapitulated in Revelation 20.

If you have not made Jesus the Lord or King over your life, now is the time. Once He comes back, it will be too late. He will still be King, but you will have to endure wrath and judgment, if you are an unbeliever. Romans 10:9 says, "that if you confess with your mouth Jesus *as* Lord, and believe in your heart that God raised Him from the dead, you will be saved;" Confess him today as Lord and King. Call "on the name of the Lord" (Joel 2:32a).

Often people say the Old Testament points forward to the cross, and the New Testament points back to the cross. While that is true in part, both testaments also point forward to the coming kingdom in its full glory. Revelation 11:15-19 is the culmination of the whole Bible.

15 Then <u>the seventh angel sounded</u>; and there were loud voices in heaven, saying, "<u>The kingdom of the world has become the kingdom of our Lord and of His Christ; and He will reign</u> forever and ever."

16 And the twenty-four elders, who sit on their thrones before God, fell on their faces and worshiped God,

17 saying, "We give You thanks, O Lord God, the Almighty, <u>who are and who were</u>, because You have taken Your great power and <u>have begun to reign.</u>

18 "And the nations were enraged, and Your <u>wrath</u> came, and the time *came* for the dead to be <u>judged</u>, and *the time* to reward Your bond-servants the prophets and the saints and those who fear Your name, the small and the great, and to destroy those who destroy the earth."

19 And the temple of God which is in heaven was opened; and the ark of His covenant appeared in His temple, and there were <u>flashes of lightning</u> and sounds and <u>peals of thunder</u> and an <u>earthquake</u> and a <u>great hailstorm</u>. (Revelation 11:15-19)

This seventh trumpet is the last trumpet. The last trumpet announces the arrival of Christ and the kingdom, and is the call for the resurrection and rapture.

> 51 Behold, I tell you a mystery; we will not all sleep, but we will all be changed,
> 52 in a moment, in the twinkling of an eye, <u>at the last trumpet</u>; for the trumpet will sound, and <u>the dead will be raised imperishable, and we will be changed</u>. (1 Corinthians 15:51-52)

In summary, Revelation 11 is not chronological, in that we are brought to the end of the end times twice; once with the two witnesses from Revelation 11:1-13, and a second time with the seventh trumpet from Revelation 11:14-19. From the outline, III. E. can be summarized as **Inferred Resurrection, Inferred Rapture, Wrath of God, Second Coming, and the 1,000 Year Reign**.

I. The things which you have seen (Revelation 1)
II. The things which are (Revelation 2-3)
III. The things which will take place after these things (Revelation 4-22)
    A. Inferred Resurrection and Rapture before the Wrath of God (Revelation 4-6)
    B. Resurrection, and Inferred Wrath of God (Revelation 7-8:1)
    C. Armageddon Starts, and the Second Coming (Revelation 8:2-10:11)
    D. Resurrection, Rapture, and Inferred Wrath of God (Revelation 11:1-11:13)
    E. Inferred Resurrection, Inferred Rapture, Wrath of God, Second Coming, and the 1,000 Year Reign (Revelation 11:14-11:19)

F. Birth of Jesus, Dragon, Woman in the Wilderness (Revelation 12:1-6)

Our 6th parallel pass through Revelation is only 6 verses, but covers thousands of years. It starts at the birth of Christ in the first century and continues through the last three-and-a-half years of Daniel's 70th seven. It includes the Dragon, who we later find out is Satan. It is good to keep in mind while studying Revelation that it is about a battle (Revelation 20:9-10) between a slain Lamb (Revelation 5:6) and a dragon (Revelation 12:4). We should not hold too tightly to literalism in apocalyptic literature. In this case, Herod personified or was empowered by the dragon.

> 16 Then when <u>Herod</u> saw that he had been tricked by the magi, he became very enraged, and sent and <u>slew all the male children who were in Bethlehem</u> and all its vicinity, from two years old and under, according to the time which he had determined from the magi. (Matthew 2:16)

> 4 And his tail swept away a third of the stars of heaven and threw them to the earth. And <u>the dragon stood before the woman who was about to give birth, so that when she gave birth he might devour her child</u>. (Revelation 12:4)

The woman, who symbolizes Israel, fled to the wilderness for the last 3.5 years of Daniel's 70th seven.

> 6 Then the woman fled into the <u>wilderness</u> where she had a place prepared by God, so that there she would be nourished for <u>one thousand two hundred and sixty days</u>. (Revelation 12:6)

This is similar to Jesus' instruction in the Olivet Discourse.

> 15 "Therefore when you see the ABOMINATION OF DESOLATION which was spoken of through Daniel the prophet, standing in the holy place (let the reader understand),
> 16 then those who are in Judea must flee to the mountains.(Matthew 24:15-16)

The abomination of desolation is at the 3.5 year marker. Jesus is telling those in Judea to flee to the mountains for 3.5 years and John is telling Israel to flee to the wilderness for 3.5 years. Presumably, those in Israel should flee to a mountainous wilderness. As you will see in the next section, while Israel is gone for 3.5 years, Satan is making war with the Christians. Therefore, this section will be labeled **Inferred Armageddon Starts**.

This section, Revelation 12:1-6, will be recapitulated in the following verses, Revelation 12:7-17.

I. The things which you have seen (Revelation 1)
II. The things which are (Revelation 2-3)
III. The things which will take place after these things (Revelation 4-22)
   A. Inferred Resurrection and Rapture before the Wrath of God (Revelation 4-6)
   B. Resurrection, and Inferred Wrath of God (Revelation 7-8:1)
   C. Armageddon Starts, and the Second Coming (Revelation 8:2-10:11)
   D. Resurrection, Rapture, Wrath of God (Revelation 11:1-11:13)

E. Inferred Resurrection, Inferred Rapture, Wrath of God, Second Coming, and the 1,000 Year Reign (Revelation 11:14-11:19)

F. Inferred Armageddon Starts (Revelation 12:1-6)

G. Dragon, Woman in the Wilderness, War with Jesus Witnesses (Revelation 12:7-17)

In Revelation 12 Michael throws down Satan from heaven, and Satan's co-consipring fallen angels (demons) come down with him. We already covered this while studying the trumpets. The woman, who we determined to be Israel in the Pre-Tribulation section of this book, flies to the wilderness for 3.5 years. Then the Dragon makes war against Christians, for only Christians "hold to the testimony of Jesus."

> 17 So the <u>dragon</u> was enraged with the woman, and went off to <u>make war</u> with the rest of her children, who keep the commandments of God and <u>hold to the testimony of Jesus</u>. (Revelation 12:17)

We end with the last three and a half years, and the start of a war against the followers of Jesus, which culminates in the battle of Armageddon. Therefore, this section will be labeled **Armageddon Starts**.

I. The things which you have seen (Revelation 1)
II. The things which are (Revelation 2-3)
III. The things which will take place after these things (Revelation 4-22)
    A. Inferred Resurrection and Rapture before the Wrath of God (Revelation 4-6)
    B. Resurrection, and Inferred Wrath of God (Revelation 7-8:1)

C. Armageddon Starts, and the Second Coming (Revelation 8:2-10:11)
D. Resurrection, Rapture, and Inferred Wrath of God (Revelation 11:1-11:13)
E. Inferred Resurrection, Inferred Rapture, Wrath of God, Second Coming, and the 1,000 Year Reign (Revelation 11:14-11:19)
F. Inferred Armageddon Starts (Revelation 12:1-6)
G. Armageddon Starts (Revelation 12:7-17)

H. Beast from the Sea, Beast from the Earth, Lamb on Mt. Zion (Revelation 13:1-14:5)

Another example to prove Revelation is not chronological comes in Revelation 14. Revelation 13:1-10, describes a beast or monster from the sea [or the Antichrist (1 John 2:18)]. While Revelation 13:11-18 describes a beast from the earth [or the false prophet (Revelation 16:13)]. Finally, Revelation 14:1-5 describes the Lamb on Mt. Zion (or Jesus). So, we are given the descriptions of a sea monster, a beast, and a Lamb. There is a common theme of using animal-like creatures to describe the major players in Revelation. There is a contrast with those marked by the beast in Revelation 13:16-18, and those marked by Jesus in Revelation 14:1. We are left with the Lamb standing on Mount Zion:

> Then I looked, and behold, the Lamb was standing on Mount Zion, and with Him one hundred and forty-four thousand, having His name and the name of His Father written on their foreheads. (Revelation 14:1)

The Lamb, Jesus, standing on Mt. Zion is a second coming passage. He has obviously come back at this point, because He is standing on earth. However, Revelation 14:1-5 is recorded several chapters before Jesus comes back on a white horse for battle.

> And I saw heaven opened, and behold, a <u>white horse</u>, and <u>He who sat on it</u> *is* <u>called Faithful and True</u>, and in righteousness He judges and wages war. (Revelation 19:11)

> And the rest were killed with the sword which came from the mouth of <u>Him who sat on the horse,</u> and all the birds were filled with their flesh. (Revelation 19:21)

Both Revelation 14:1-5, and Revelation 19:11-21 describe Jesus' second coming in different ways for different purposes. In Revelation 19 Jesus is described as a warrior saving the world, and in Revelation 14 as a Lamb who saved the world.

I.   The things which you have seen (Revelation 1)
II. The things which are (Revelation 2-3)
III. The things which will take place after these things (Revelation 4-22)
   A. Inferred Resurrection and Rapture before the Wrath of God (Revelation 4-6)
   B. Resurrection, and Inferred Wrath of God (Revelation 7-8:1)
   C. Armageddon Starts, and the Second Coming (Revelation 8:2-10:11)
   D. Resurrection, Rapture, and Inferred Wrath of God (Revelation 11:1-11:13)
   E. Inferred Resurrection, Inferred Rapture, Wrath of God, Second Coming, and the 1,000 Year Reign (Revelation 11:14-11:19)

F. Inferred Armageddon Starts (Revelation 12:1-6)

G. Armageddon Starts (Revelation 12:7-17)

H. Second Coming (Revelation 13:1-14:5)

I. 3 Angels' Announcements, 2 Reapings (Revelation 14:6-20)

While the rapture has been inferred in Revelation 6:14, Revelation 7:9, and Revelation 11:15, it is most clearly seen in Revelation 14:14-16.

> 14 Then I looked, and behold, a <u>white cloud</u>, and sitting on the cloud *was* one like a <u>son of man</u>, having a <u>golden crown</u> on His head and a sharp sickle in His hand.
> 15 And another angel came out of the temple, crying out with a loud voice to Him who sat on the cloud, "Put in your sickle and reap, <u>for the hour to reap has come</u>, because the <u>harvest of the earth is ripe</u>."
> 16 Then He who sat on the cloud swung His sickle over the earth, and <u>the earth was reaped</u>.
> (Revelation 14:14-16)

This rapture passage in Revelation 14:14-16 chronologically comes before the Lamb is standing on Mt. Zion in Revelation 14:1-5. This is a great example of recapitulation. One section brought us to the end of the story in Revelation 14:5, then this section brings us to the end again in a different manner. There is an unfortunate, and uninspired chapter boundary at Revelation 14:1. It would make more sense to put Revelation 14:1-5 in chapter 13, then start Revelation 14 at verse 6. While this section includes the rapture (at the first reaping), it also includes the wrath of God (at the second reaping), as each of the other rapture passages also include the wrath of God after the rapture, Revelation 6:16, Revelation 8:1 (inferred), and Revelation 11:18.

> 16 and they said to the mountains and to the rocks, "Fall on us and hide us from the presence of Him who sits on the throne, and from the <u>wrath of the Lamb</u>; (Revelation 6:16)

> 1 When the Lamb broke the seventh seal, there was <u>silence</u> in heaven for about <u>half an hour</u>. (Revelation 8:1)

> 18 "And the nations were enraged, and <u>Your wrath came</u>, and the time *came* for the dead to be judged, and *the time* to reward Your bond-servants the prophets and the saints and those who fear Your name, the small and the great, and to destroy those who destroy the earth." (Revelation 11:18)

> 19 So the angel swung his sickle to the earth and gathered *the clusters from* the vine of the earth, and <u>threw them into the great wine press of the wrath of God</u>. (Revelation 14:19)

This section includes the resurrection, the rapture, the wrath of God, the end of Armageddon, and the second coming.

> 20 And the <u>wine press was trodden</u> outside the city, and blood came out from the wine press, up to the horses' bridles, for a distance of two hundred miles. (Revelation 14:20)

> 15 From His mouth comes a sharp sword, so that with it He may strike down the nations, and He

will rule them with a rod of iron; and <u>He treads the wine press of the fierce wrath of God, the Almighty</u>. (Revelation 19:15)

I. The things which you have seen (Revelation 1)
II. The things which are (Revelation 2-3)
III. The things which will take place after these things (Revelation 4-22)
    A. Inferred Resurrection and Rapture before the Wrath of God (Revelation 4-6)
    B. Resurrection, and Inferred Wrath of God (Revelation 7-8:1)
    C. Armageddon Starts, and the Second Coming (Revelation 8:2-10:11)
    D. Resurrection, Rapture, and Inferred Wrath of God (Revelation 11:1-11:13)
    E. Inferred Resurrection, Inferred Rapture, Wrath of God, Second Coming, and the 1,000 Year Reign (Revelation 11:14-11:19)
    F. Inferred Armageddon Starts (Revelation 12:1-6)
    G. Armageddon Starts (Revelation 12:7-17)
    H. Second Coming (Revelation 13:1-14:5)
    I. Resurrection, Rapture, Wrath of God, Armageddon Ends, Second Coming (Revelation 14:6-20)

J. 7 Bowls of the Wrath of God, Lightning Thunder Earthquake and Hail (Revelation 15-16)

Chapters 15 and 16 of Revelation are about the seven bowls of the wrath of God. While God's wrath was alluded to in Revelation 6:16, Revelation 8:1 (inferred), Revelation 11:18, and Revelation 14:19, it is recapitulated in great detail in Revelation 16. This passage also has the start of Armageddon.

16 And they gathered them together to the place which in Hebrew is called Har-Magedon. (Revelation 16:16)

The section concludes with the lightning, thunder, earthquake, and hail we have seen in other parallel accounts.

> 12 I looked when He broke the sixth seal, and there was a <u>great earthquake</u>; and the sun became black as sackcloth *made* of hair, and the whole moon became like blood;
> 13 and the stars of the sky fell to the earth, as a fig tree casts its unripe figs when shaken by a great wind.
> 14 The sky was split apart like a scroll when it is rolled up, and <u>every mountain and island were moved out of their places</u>. (Revelation 6:12-14)

> 3 and he cried out with a loud voice, as when a lion roars; and when he had cried out, the <u>seven peals of thunder</u> uttered their voices.
> 4 When the <u>seven peals of thunder had spoken</u>, I was about to write; and I heard a voice from heaven saying, "Seal up the things which the <u>seven peals of thunder</u> have spoken and do not write them." (Revelation 10:3-4)

> 13 And in that hour there was a <u>great earthquake</u>, and a tenth of the city fell; seven thousand people were killed in the earthquake, and the rest were terrified and gave glory to the God of heaven. (Revelation 11:13)

19 And the temple of God which is in heaven was opened; and the ark of His covenant appeared in His temple, and there were flashes of <u>lightning</u> and sounds and <u>peals of thunder</u> and an <u>earthquake</u> and a <u>great hailstorm</u>. (Revelation 11:13)

18 And there were flashes of <u>lightning</u> and sounds and peals of <u>thunder</u>; and there was a <u>great earthquake</u>, such as there had not been since man came to be upon the earth, so <u>great an earthquake</u> *was it, and* so mighty.
19 The great city was split into three parts, and the cities of the nations fell. Babylon the great was remembered before God, to give her the cup of the wine of His fierce wrath.
20 And <u>every island fled away, and the mountains were not found</u>.
21 And huge <u>hailstones,</u> about one hundred pounds each, came down from heaven upon men; and men blasphemed God because of the plague of the hail, because its plague was extremely severe. (Revelation 16:20-21)

Revelation 15-16 includes the wrath of God, and start of Armageddon.

I. The things which you have seen (Revelation 1)
II. The things which are (Revelation 2-3)
III. The things which will take place after these things (Revelation 4-22)
    A. Inferred Resurrection and Rapture before the Wrath of God (Revelation 4-6)

B. Resurrection, and Inferred Wrath of God (Revelation 7-8:1)

C. Armageddon Starts, and the Second Coming (Revelation 8:2-10:11)

D. Resurrection, Rapture, and Inferred Wrath of God (Revelation 11:1-11:13)

E. Inferred Resurrection, Inferred Rapture, Wrath of God, Second Coming, and the 1,000 Year Reign (Revelation 11:14-11:19)

F. Inferred Armageddon Starts (Revelation 12:1-6)

G. Armageddon Starts (Revelation 12:7-17)

H. Second Coming (Revelation 13:1-14:5)

I. Resurrection, Rapture, Wrath of God, Armageddon Ends, Second Coming (Revelation 14:6-20)

J. Wrath of God, Armageddon Starts, Armageddon Ends (Revelation 15-16)

K. Babylon, Thunder, Coming of the King, 1,000 Years (Revelation 17:1-20:3)

When people start to study Revelation they usually wonder how the United States of America factors into Revelation. I do not know if the United States is in Revelation, but if you want to find out what happens to a people like the U.S., read Revelation 18. that chapter is preceded by Revelation 17 that explains some of the symbolism in Revelation. Chapter 18, also includes the rapture, as a heavenly voice calls out His people:

> 4 I heard another voice from heaven, saying, "Come out of her, my people, so that you will not participate in her sins and receive of her plagues; (Revelation 18:4)

The 19th chapter is another recapitulation of the second coming of Christ. We have already seen Him come in Revelation 10:1-2, Revelation 11:15-17, and Revelation 14:1.

> 1 I saw another strong angel <u>coming down out of heaven</u>, clothed with a <u>cloud;</u> and the <u>rainbow</u> was upon his head, and his <u>face was like the sun</u>, and his <u>feet like pillars of fire;</u>
> 2 and he had in his hand a little book which was open. He placed his <u>right foot on the sea</u> and <u>his left on the land;</u> (Revelation 10:1-2)

> 15 Then the seventh angel sounded; and there were loud voices in heaven, saying, "<u>The kingdom of the world has become *the kingdom* of our Lord and of His Christ</u>; and He will reign forever and ever."
> 16 And the twenty-four elders, who sit on their thrones before God, fell on their faces and worshiped God,
> 17 saying, "We give You thanks, O Lord God, the Almighty, <u>who are and who were</u>, because You have taken Your great power and <u>have begun to reign</u>. (Revelation 11:15-17)

> 1 Then I looked, and behold, <u>the Lamb was standing on Mount Zion</u>, and with Him one hundred and forty-four thousand, having His name and the name of His Father written on their foreheads. (Revelation 14:1)

> 20 And the <u>wine press was trodden outside the city</u>, and blood came out from the wine press, up

to the horses' bridles, for a distance of two hundred miles. (Revelation 14:20)

11 And I saw heaven opened, and behold, a white horse, and <u>He who sat on it *is* called Faithful and True</u>, and in righteousness He judges and wages war. (Revelation 19:20)

Revelation 19 is an awesome chapter about the Lords return. Revelation 19:6, and 16, along with Revelation 11:15 are the lyrics used in the Hallelujah Chorus, from *Handel's Messiah*.

15 And the seventh angel sounded; and there were great voices in heaven, saying, <u>The kingdoms of this world are become *the kingdoms* of our Lord, and of his Christ; and he shall reign for ever and ever.</u> (Revelation 11:15 KJV)

6 And I heard as it were the voice of a great multitude, and as the voice of many waters, and as the voice of mighty thunderings, saying, <u>Alleluia: for the Lord God omnipotent reigneth.</u> (Revelation 19:6 KJV)

16 And he hath on *his* vesture and on his thigh a name written, <u>KING OF KINGS, AND LORD OF LORDS.</u> (Revelation 19:16 KJV)

This section ends with the end of Armageddon in Revelation 19:19-21, and the 1,000 years in Revelation 20:3.

19 And I saw the beast and the kings of the earth and their <u>armies</u> assembled <u>to make war</u> against Him who sat on the horse and <u>against His army</u>.

20 And the beast was seized, and with him the false prophet who performed the signs in his presence, by which he deceived those who had received the mark of the beast and those who worshiped his image; these two were thrown alive into the lake of fire which burns with brimstone. 21 And <u>the rest were killed with the sword</u> which came from the mouth of Him who sat on the horse, and all the birds were filled with their flesh. (Revelation 19:19-21)

3 and he threw him into the abyss, and shut *it* and sealed *it* over him, so that he would not deceive the nations any longer, <u>until the thousand years were completed</u>; after these things he must be released for a short time. (Revelation 20:3)

Revelation 17:1-20:3 can be summarized with **Rapture, Second Coming, Armageddon Ends, and 1,000 years.**

I. The things which you have seen (Revelation 1)
II. The things which are (Revelation 2-3)
III. The things which will take place after these things (Revelation 4-22)
   A. Inferred Resurrection and Rapture before the Wrath of God (Revelation 4-6)
   B. Resurrection, and Inferred Wrath of God (Revelation 7-8:1)
   C. Armageddon Starts, and the Second Coming (Revelation 8:2-10:11)
   D. Resurrection, Rapture, and Inferred Wrath of God (Revelation 11:1-11:13)

E. Inferred Resurrection, Inferred Rapture, Wrath of God, Second Coming, and the 1,000 Year Reign (Revelation 11:14-11:19)
F. Inferred Armageddon Starts (Revelation 12:1-6)
G. Armageddon Starts (Revelation 12:7-17)
H. Second Coming (Revelation 13:1-14:5)
I. Resurrection, Rapture, Wrath of God, Armageddon Ends, Second Coming (Revelation 14:6-20)
J. Wrath of God, Armageddon Starts, Armageddon Ends (Revelation 15-16)
K. Rapture, Second Coming, Armageddon Ends, 1,000 years (Revelation 17:1-20:3)

L. 1,000 Years, Great White Throne, New: Heaven, Earth, Jerusalem (Revelation 20:4-22:21)

The final section includes mostly new material about the 1,000 year reign, the Great White Throne Judgment, the New Heaven, New Earth, and New Jerusalem. The resurrection is frequently recapitulated in Revelation 6:14, Revelation 7:9, Revelation 11:15, and Revelation 14:14-16. It is described again in Revelation 20:4-6 quite explicitly.

> 4 Then I saw thrones, and they sat on them, and judgment was given to them. And I *saw* the souls of those who had been beheaded because of their testimony of Jesus and because of the word of God, and those who had not worshiped the beast or his image, and had not received the mark on their forehead and on their hand; and they came to life and reigned with Christ for a thousand years.
> 5 The rest of the dead did not come to life until the

thousand years were completed. <u>This is the first resurrection.</u>

6 Blessed and holy is the one who has a part in the <u>first resurrection</u>; over these the <u>second death</u> has no power, but they will be priests of God and of Christ and will <u>reign with Him for a thousand years</u>. (Revelation 20:4-6)

In addition to describing the resurrection, John mentions the second death in Revelation 20:6. We later find out that the second death is the lake of fire.

14 Then death and Hades were thrown into the lake of fire. <u>This is the second death, the lake of fire</u>. (Revelation 20:14)

Paul says in Romans 6:23, "For the wages of sin is death." It is the second death that Paul is speaking of. Our wages are what we earn. Sin is missing God's target in the way He wants us to live. In other words, if we miss God's target, we earn the lake of fire. Thankfully the verse does not stop there, "but the free gift of God is eternal life in Christ Jesus our Lord." By accepting God's free gift, we do not need to go to the lake of fire, we get to live again with Jesus forever. There is a catchy phrase that says, "Believers die once to live twice, unbelievers live once to die twice." If you have not accepted God's forgiveness, please do so right now. Talk to God, the Judge. Tell Him you are sorry you have missed His target, and that you would like to receive His free gift of eternal life.

23 For the <u>wages of sin is death</u>, but the <u>free gift of God is eternal life</u> in Christ Jesus our Lord. (Romans 6:23)

The fact that God's Holy Spirit through John brings us to the end of the age about twelve times, proves that Revelation is not chronological. We can see John uses recapitulation to describe the same period of time from different perspectives. While assuming Revelation is chronological was once logical, now we know it is not. Knowing this, we should get in to the habit of asking, for each passage in Revelation, has the story started over again? The following page is a timeline, illustrating when each section of revelation starts and stops.

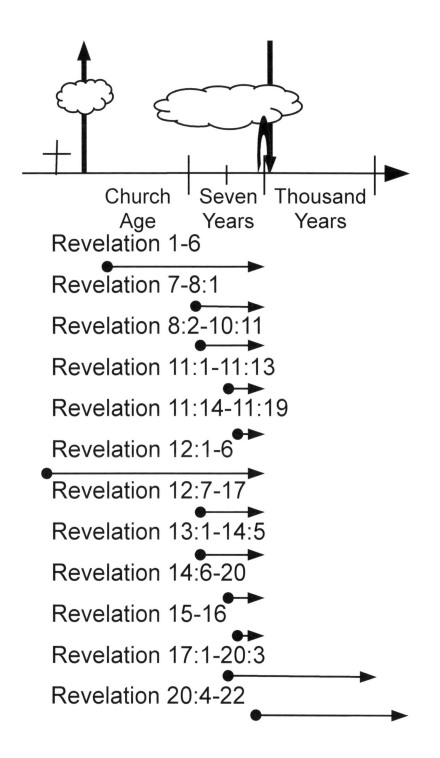

Church Age | Seven Years | Thousand Years

Revelation 1-6

Revelation 7-8:1

Revelation 8:2-10:11

Revelation 11:1-11:13

Revelation 11:14-11:19

Revelation 12:1-6

Revelation 12:7-17

Revelation 13:1-14:5

Revelation 14:6-20

Revelation 15-16

Revelation 17:1-20:3

Revelation 20:4-22

Below is the revised outline, this time highlighting which of the major events (resurrection, rapture, wrath of God, Armageddon Starts, Second Coming, Armageddon Ends, and the 1,000 Year Reign) are alluded to.

I.   The things which you have seen (Revelation 1)
II. The things which are (Revelation 2-3)
III. The things which will take place after these things (Revelation 4-22)
    A. Inferred Resurrection and Rapture before the Wrath of God (Revelation 4-6)
    B. Resurrection, and Inferred Wrath of God (Revelation 7-8:1)
    C. Armageddon Starts, and the Second Coming (Revelation 8:2-10:11)
    D. Resurrection, Rapture, and Inferred Wrath of God (Revelation 11:1-11:13)
    E. Inferred Resurrection, Inferred Rapture, Wrath of God, Second Coming, and the 1,000 Year Reign (Revelation 11:14-11:19)
    F. Inferred Armageddon Starts (Revelation 12:1-6)
    G. Armageddon Starts (Revelation 12:7-17)
    H. Second Coming (Revelation 13:1-14:5)
    I. Resurrection, Rapture, Wrath of God, Armageddon Ends, Second Coming (Revelation 14:6-20)
    J. Wrath of God, Armageddon Starts, Armageddon Ends (Revelation 15-16)
    K. Rapture, Second Coming, Armageddon Ends, 1,000 years (Revelation 17:1-20:3)
    L. Resurrection, 1,000 Year Reign (Revelation 20:4-22:21)

We have seen that Revelation is not chronological. John cycles through the end time events repeatedly, each time giving a different recap of the last days. This recapitulation is the key to merging together the best defenses of each of the rapture views.

How is Recapitulation used in Rapture Fusion?

Now, let's take the best ideas from each of the four major Pre-Millennial rapture views and use recapitulation to fuse them together. We will not necessarily use the ideas that a person of each view would say are best, but the ideas that fit with scripture best and form a better system and explanation of end time events.

Merger of Traditional Rapture Views

Best Features:	Provided By:	Scripture:
Seven Year Tribulation	Pre-Tribulation	Daniel 9:27
Rapture before the wrath of God	Pre-Tribulation	1 Thessalonians 1:10, 5:9
Rapture at the seventh trumpet	Mid-Tribulation	1 Corinthians 15:51-52, Revelation 11:15-17
Seven trumpets starting before the middle of the tribulation	Mid-Tribulation	Revelation 8-11
6th Seal celestial disturbances match Jesus' rapture prerequisites	Pre-Wrath	Revelation 6:12-14 Matthew 24:29-31
Wrath of God starts after the 6th seal is opened	Pre-Wrath	Revelation 6:15-17
Only one second coming	Post-Tribulation	Hebrews 9:28
Only one first resurrection	Post-Tribulation	Revelation 20:4-6

The Pre-Tribulation view provides the framework of a seven year tribulation before Christ comes back to earth. The Pre-Trib rapture position really brought the seven year tribulation to the forefront of the rapture debate. This comes from Daniel 9:27

27 The ruler will make a treaty with the people for a period of <u>one set of seven</u>, but after <u>half this time</u>, he will put an end to the sacrifices and offerings. And as a climax to all his terrible deeds, he will set up a sacrilegious object that causes desecration, until the fate decreed for this defiler is finally poured out on him." (Daniel 9:27 NLT).

The ruler (or Antichrist) will make a seven-year treaty with the many. This will kick off the prophetic stopwatch for the seven-year tribulation. Mid way through, at the 3.5-year marker, the Antichrist will set up the abomination of desolation. After seven years have passed since the treaty was made, Christ will return to earth.

The Pre-Tribulation position also stresses that Christians will not have to endure the wrath of God.

10 and to wait for His Son from heaven, whom He raised from the dead, *that is* <u>Jesus</u>, who <u>rescues us from</u> the <u>wrath</u> to come. (1 Thessalonians 1:10)

9 For <u>God has not destined us for wrath</u>, but for obtaining salvation through our Lord Jesus Christ, (1 Thessalonians 5:9)

This begs the question, when in the seven-year tribulation does God's wrath start?

This is where we fuse in the Pre-Wrath view. The Pre-Wrath view holds that the wrath starts after the sixth seal is opened, namely Revelation 6:16. Pre-Wrath also highlights the 6th Seal celestial disturbances which match Jesus' rapture prerequisites. However, the wrath of God starts at each of the following passages: Revelation 6:16, Revelation 8:1 (in conjunction with

Revelation 15:8), Revelation 11:13 (in conjunction with Revelation 16:18-19), Revelation 11:18, Revelation 14:19, Revelation 16:1, and Revelation 20:15 (in conjunction with Romans 2:5).

Let's take each of the Revelation wrath passages one at a time. The mention of the word wrath is in Revelation 6:16 after the sixth seal is broken. Since God's wrath is such an important topic in Revelation and the rapture, it is easy to surmise that the first five seals were not God's wrath, because God did not call them wrath. God was removing His seals of protection, but not inflicting wrath until after the sixth seal is broken.

> 16 and they said to the mountains and to the rocks, "Fall on us and hide us from the presence of Him who sits on the throne, and from the <u>wrath of the Lamb</u>; (Revelation 6:16)

The next instance of God's wrath is at the seventh seal. Wrath is not specifically mentioned, but can be inferred from those who wanted to be saved from the wrath of the Lamb when they saw Jesus at the end of the sixth seal. As I previously mentioned, the silence probably occurs as the seven bowls of the wrath of God are poured out when "no one was able to enter the temple" (Revelation 15:8) thus creating the silence.

> 1 When the Lamb broke the seventh seal, there was <u>silence in heaven</u> for about half an hour. (Revelation 8:1)

After the seals, wrath is not mentioned during the first six trumpets, not until the end of the interlude in Revelation 11:13, at the end of the seven year tribulation.

13 And in that hour there was a great earthquake, and a tenth of the city fell; seven thousand people were killed in the earthquake, and the rest were terrified and gave glory to the God of heaven. (Revelation 11:13)

18 And there were flashes of lightning and sounds and peals of thunder; and there was a great earthquake, such as there had not been since man came to be upon the earth, so great an earthquake *was it, and* so mighty.
19 The great city was split into three parts, and the cities of the nations fell. Babylon the great was remembered before God, to give her the cup of the wine of His fierce wrath. (Revelation 16:18-19)

18 "And the nations were enraged, and Your wrath came, and the time *came* for the dead to be judged, and *the time* to reward Your bond-servants the prophets and the saints and those who fear Your name, the small and the great, and to destroy those who destroy the earth." (Revelation 11:18)

19 So the angel swung his sickle to the earth and gathered *the clusters from* the vine of the earth, and threw them into the great wine press of the wrath of God. (Revelation 14:19)

1 Then I heard a loud voice from the temple, saying to the seven angels, "Go and pour out on the earth the seven bowls of the wrath of God." (Revelation 16:1)

8 "For this reason in one day her plagues will come, <u>pestilence</u> and <u>mourning</u> and <u>famine,</u> and she will be <u>burned up with fire</u>; for the <u>Lord God who judges</u> her is strong. (Revelation 18:8)

15 And if anyone's name was not found written in the book of life, he was <u>thrown into the lake of fire</u>.(Revelation 20:15)

5 But because of your stubbornness and unrepentant heart you are storing up wrath for yourself in <u>the day of wrath</u> and <u>revelation of the righteous judgment of God,</u> (Romans 2:5)

We can line those verses up using recapitulation and see that they are all talking about the same wrathful event.

While the Pre-Trib view says the rapture takes place before the wrath of God, the Pre-Wrath view says the rapture happens after the sun and moon are darkened and the stars fall, and the Mid-Trib view says the rapture happens at the 7th trumpet. When we fuse in the Mid-Tribulation view that the rapture happens at the seventh trumpet, we can correlate the seventh trumpet with the 6th seal. The Mid-Tribulation view also allows us to start the trumpets before the seals are finished.

We can do a similar exercise with the resurrection and rapture passages that we did with the wrath of God passages. The following are the resurrection and rapture passages in Revelation, Revelation 6:12-14 (in conjunction with Matthew 24:29-31), Revelation 7:9 (in conjunction with Revelation 6:9-11), Revelation 11:12, Revelation 11:15-17 (in conjunction with 1 Corinthians 15:51-52), Revelation 14:14-16, Revelation 15:1-3, Revelation 18:4 and Revelation 20:4-6.

12 I looked when He broke the sixth seal, and there was a great earthquake; and the sun became black as sackcloth *made* of hair, and the whole moon became like blood;
13 and the stars of the sky fell to the earth, as a fig tree casts its unripe figs when shaken by a great wind.
14 The sky was split apart like a scroll when it is rolled up, and every mountain and island were moved out of their places. (Revelation 6:12-14)

29 "But immediately after the tribulation of those days THE SUN WILL BE DARKENED, AND THE MOON WILL NOT GIVE ITS LIGHT, AND THE STARS WILL FALL from the sky, and the powers of the heavens will be shaken.
30 "And then the sign of the Son of Man will appear in the sky, and then all the tribes of the earth will mourn, and they will see the SON OF MAN COMING ON THE CLOUDS OF THE SKY with power and great glory.
31 "And He will send forth His angels with A GREAT TRUMPET and THEY WILL GATHER TOGETHER His elect from the four winds, from one end of the sky to the other (Matthew 24:29-31)

9 After these things I looked, and behold, a great multitude which no one could count, from every nation and *all* tribes and peoples and tongues, standing before the throne and before the Lamb, clothed in white robes, and palm branches *were* in their hands; (Revelation 7:9)

9 When the Lamb broke the fifth seal, I saw underneath the altar the souls of those who had been slain because of the word of God, and because of the testimony which they had maintained;

10 and they cried out with a loud voice, saying, "How long, O Lord, holy and true, will You refrain from judging and avenging our blood on those who dwell on the earth?"

11 And there was given to each of them a white robe; and they were told that they should rest for a little while longer, until *the number of* their fellow servants and their brethren who were to be killed even as they had been, would be completed also. (Revelation 6:9-11)

12 And they heard a loud voice from heaven saying to them, "Come up here." Then they went up into heaven in the cloud, and their enemies watched them. (Revelation 11:12)

15 Then the seventh angel sounded; and there were loud voices in heaven, saying, "The kingdom of the world has become the kingdom of our Lord and of His Christ; and He will reign forever and ever."

16 And the twenty-four elders, who sit on their thrones before God, fell on their faces and worshiped God,

17 saying, "We give You thanks, O Lord God, the Almighty, who are and who were, because You have taken Your great power and have begun to reign. (Revelation 11:15-17)

51 Behold, I tell you a mystery; we will not all sleep, but <u>we will all be changed</u>,
52 in a moment, in the twinkling of an eye, <u>at the last trumpet</u>; for <u>the trumpet will sound</u>, and the <u>dead will be raised</u> imperishable, and <u>we will be changed</u>. (1 Corinthians 15:51-52)

14 Then I looked, and behold, <u>a white cloud</u>, and sitting on the cloud *was* one like a <u>son of man</u>, having a <u>golden crown</u> on His head and a sharp sickle in His hand.
15 And another angel came out of the temple, crying out with a loud voice to Him who sat on the cloud, "<u>Put in your sickle and reap</u>, for the hour to reap has come, because <u>the harvest of the earth is ripe</u>."
16 Then He who sat on the cloud swung His sickle over the earth, and <u>the earth was reaped</u>. (Revelation 14:14-16)

1 Then I saw another sign <u>in heaven [the sky]</u>, great and marvelous, seven angels who had seven plagues, *which are* the last, because in them the wrath of God is finished.
2 And I saw something like a sea of glass mixed with fire, and <u>those who had been victorious</u> over the beast and his image and the number of his name, standing on the sea of glass, holding harps of God. (Revelation 15:1-2)

4 I heard another voice from heaven, saying, "<u>Come out of her, my people</u>, so that you will not

participate in her sins and receive of her plagues; (Revelation 18:4)

4 Then I saw thrones, and they sat on them, and judgment was given to them. And I saw the souls of those who had been beheaded because of their testimony of Jesus and because of the word of God, and those who had not worshiped the beast or his image, and had not received the mark on their forehead and on their hand; and they came to life and reigned with Christ for a thousand years.
5 The rest of the dead did not come to life until the thousand years were completed. This is the first resurrection.
6 Blessed and holy is the one who has a part in the first resurrection; over these the second death has no power, but they will be priests of God and of Christ and will reign with Him for a thousand years. (Revelation 20:4-6)

These last verses (Revelation 20:4-6) point out that the first resurrection is before the 1,000 years and coincides with Christ's reigning which starts at the 7th trumpet, in Revelation 11:15-17 (see above). This allows us to fuse in the best of the Post-Tribulation view, only one first resurrection at the end of the tribulation (Matthew 24:29-31). The Pre-Trib and Mid-Trib views require two 1st resurrections. One is placed at their views time for the rapture, and a second first resurrection is required at the end of the tribulation for all those who come to Christ after their rapture, but before the second 1st resurrection. As George Müller said, "If you can show me a trumpet after the last, and a resurrection before the first, then I can believe this new [Pre-Trib] doctrine." The Post-Trib structure makes the 1st resurrection much more logical, with only one first resurrection for believers. The second resurrection is the second death for unbelievers.

> 14 Then death and Hades were thrown into the lake of fire. <u>This is the second death, the lake of fire</u>. (Revelation 20:14)

Likewise, the Post-Tribulation view allows for only one second coming of Jesus (Hebrews 9:28). There is not a first second coming in the clouds at the rapture, then another second coming to Earth at the end of the tribulation. The Post-Tribulation view makes the second coming much more logical, with only one coming, where we meet Him in the Clouds on His way down to Earth. So we can fuse in only one second coming. The most clear rapture passage instructs us that the rapture and resurrection in the clouds happens at the coming of the Lord.

> 15 For this we say to you by the word of the Lord, that we who are alive and remain until <u>the coming of the Lord,</u> will not precede those who have fallen asleep.
> 16 For the Lord Himself will descend from heaven with a shout, with the voice of the archangel and with the trumpet of God, and <u>the dead in Christ will rise first</u>.
> 17 <u>Then we who are alive and remain will be caught up</u> together with them <u>in the clouds</u> to meet the Lord in the air, and so we shall always be with the Lord. (1 Thessalonians 4:15-17)

Let's align the resurrection/rapture events with the wrath events.

Event	Resurrection/Rapture Passage	Wrath Passage
6th Seal	Revelation 6:12-14 (inferred from Matthew 24:29-31)	Revelation 6:16
Interlude – 7th Seal	Revelation 7:9 (inferred from Revelation 6:9-11)	Revelation 8:1 (inferred from Revelation 15:8)
2 Witnesses	Revelation 11:12	Revelation 11:13 (inferred from Revelation 16:18-19)
7th Trumpet	Revelation 11:15-17 (inferred from 1 Corinthians 15:51-52)	Revelation 11:18
2 Reapings	Revelation 14:14-16	Revelation 14:19
7 Bowls of Wrath	Revelation 15:1-2	Revelation 16:1
Fall of Babylon	Revelation 18:4	Revelation 18:8
1,000 Years, Great White Throne	Revelation 20:4-6	Revelation 20:15 (inferred from Romans 2:5)

It should be plain to see there is a close correlation between the resurrection/rapture and the wrath of God, as we would expect from 1 Thessalonians 1:10 and 1 Thessalonians 5:9. The chart also shows that the resurrection and rapture are described in many places, and in many ways, in Revelation. Hopefully this exercise makes it clear that recapitulation is not being forced on the text, but that the text would not make sense without recapitulation.

The order of events from Revelation, in chronological order, appears to start with the first trumpet (Revelation 8:7), so the 144,000 can be sealed before the seals of the scroll are broken. The first trumpet warns of the four angels bent on harm (Revelation 7:1-3). Then, seals 1 through 4 are removed (Revelation 6:1-8), ushering in the four horsemen of the apocalypse during the first half of the seven year tribulation, aligning with Matthew 24:4-15. Before the middle of the tribulation, trumpets 2-5 are sounded (Revelation 8:8-9:12), allowing Satan to exercise his great wrath for the last three-and-a-half years (Revelation 12:12-14). This allows for the Antichrist and the False Prophet to be the focus of the abomination of desolation. I suspect the fifth seal is broken (Revelation 6:9-11) near the middle of the seven year tribulation. The sixth trumpet (Revelation 9:13-21) starts Armageddon, and is interrupted with the sixth seal (Revelation 6:12-14), immediately followed by the seventh and last trumpet (Revelation 11:15-17). The sixth seal has to happen after the abomination of desolation to align with Matthew 24:15-31. Likewise, the seventh trumpet has to be blown after Armageddon starts, and signals the end of the tribulation. When the seventh trumpet is blown (1 Corinthians 15:51-52, Revelation 11:15-17) the resurrection and rapture take place, after the tribulation (Matthew 24:29), which is after the sixth seal is opened (Matthew 24:29-31, Revelation 6:12). While believers are meeting Christ in the clouds, the seven bowls of the wrath of God are poured out (Revelation 16) during the half hour of silence from the seventh seal (Revelation 8:1). Upon completion of the bowls, and with Christ's return, there are seven peals of thunder (Revelation 10:1-4). When Christ returns to earth with his army in toe, He finishes Armageddon (Revelation 19:20-21), and stands victorious with His 144,000 (Revelation 14:1-5). Then begins the 1,000 year reign (Revelation 20:4-6). In summary, the rapture happens after the tribulation, at the seventh trumpet, between the sixth and seventh seals, and before the seven bowls of the wrath of God are poured out.

The following illustration shows the events at the end of the seven year tribulation. The blowing of the sixth trumpet, followed by the opening of the sixth seal, then the seventh trumpet, followed by the seventh seal and the seven bowls of the wrath of God. Jesus coming to the clouds at the seventh trumpet, while believers (both raptured and resurrected) meet Jesus in the clouds, concurrently the seven bowls of the wrath of God are poured out. Then, Jesus continues His return from the clouds to the earth with the believers in toe.

Coming of Jesus and the Rapture

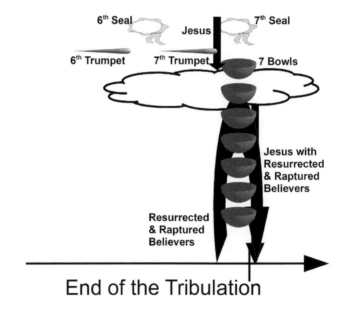

While not every aspect of every traditional rapture view can be fused together, with Rapture Fusion we can see that all of the following statements can be true at the same time. There will be a seven year tribulation. The rapture occurs before the wrath of God, and at the seventh trumpet. The seven trumpets start before the middle of the tribulation. The sixth seal celestial disturbances match Jesus' rapture prerequisites. The wrath of God starts after the sixth seal is opened. There is only one second coming, only one first resurrection, and only one last trumpet.

I believe the line "And, Lord haste the day when the faith shall be sight, The clouds be rolled back as a scroll, The trump shall resound and the Lord shall descend" in the hymn *It Is Well with My Soul* highlights the recapitulation in Revelation. The "clouds be rolled back as a scroll," is from the sixth seal (Revelation 6:14), the "trump shall resound" is the seventh trumpet (Revelation 11:15). The "Lord shall descend," can be explicitly seen in Revelation 19. The hymn is a good word picture of the simultaneous events during the return of our Lord.

Part IV:
Reexamining the Pre-Millennial Rapture Views

In light of the new timeline achieved by Rapture Fusion, let's reexamine each of the Pre-Millennial rapture views.

Reexamining the Post-Tribulation Rapture

Previously, I provided three aspects of the Post-Tribulation view:

1. Only one second-coming (Hebrews 9:28)
2. Only one first resurrection (Revelation 20:4-6)
3. The rapture will take place before the wrath of God (1 Thessalonians 5:9)

All three aspects are included in Rapture Fusion. The first two were specifically taken from the Post-Trib view, and the third is shared by all of the rapture views, in one way or another.

There will only be one second-coming, though it is spoken of many times and in many ways in Revelation. There is no evidence that the second coming will be split into two segments, one to the clouds, and one to the earth, separated by at least five months (Pre-Wrath), three and a half years (Mid-Trib), or seven years (Pre-Trib). We are clearly told Jesus will come back in the same way he went up, which was only once.

9 And after He had said these things, <u>He was lifted up</u> while they were looking on, and <u>a cloud received Him</u> out of their sight.

10 And as they were gazing intently into the sky while He was going, behold, two men in white clothing stood beside them.

11 They also said, "Men of Galilee, why do you stand looking into the sky? This Jesus, who has been taken up from you into heaven, <u>will come in just the same way as you have watched Him go into heaven.</u>" (Acts 1:9-11)

By definition, there is only one first resurrection. The first resurrection takes place after the mark of the beast. The mark is placed in the latter half of the seven year tribulation. Therefore, the first resurrection cannot take place Pre-Tribulation, nor Mid-Tribulation.

4 Then I saw thrones, and they sat on them, and judgment was given to them. And I *saw* the souls of those who had been beheaded because of their testimony of Jesus and because of the word of God, and those <u>who had not worshiped the beast or his image,</u> and <u>had not received the mark on their forehead and on their hand;</u> and <u>they came to life</u> and reigned with Christ for a thousand years.

5 The rest of the dead did not come to life until the thousand years were completed. <u>This is the first resurrection.</u> (Revelation 20:4-5)

Finally, the rapture will take place before the wrath of God. While Post-Tribulation is partially correct, it does not provide a complete picture. The Post-Tribulation view correctly identifies the seven bowls as the wrath of God, but does not traditionally fuse them together with the wrath described after the sixth seal, and after the seventh trumpet. Using the recapitulation of Rapture Fusion, we saw the rapture takes place after the sixth seal is opened (Revelation 6:12-17), before the wrath of Him who sits on the throne (Revelation 6:16), and that wrath is the seven bowls of the wrath of God (Revelation 15-16). That same wrath is also mentioned after the seventh trumpet (Revelation 11:18). The seventh trumpet is blown between the sixth and seventh seals, and is followed by the seven bowls of the wrath of God.

> 16 and they said to the mountains and to the rocks, "Fall on us and hide us from the presence of <u>Him who sits on the throne, and from the wrath of the Lamb;</u>
> 17 for the great day of <u>their wrath has come,</u> and who is able to stand?" (Revelation 6:16-17)

> 18 "And the nations were enraged, and <u>Your wrath came,</u> and the time *came* for the dead to be judged, and *the time* to reward Your bond-servants the prophets and the saints and those who fear Your name, the small and the great, and to destroy those who destroy the earth." (Revelation 11:18)

> 7 Then one of the four living creatures gave to the seven angels <u>seven golden bowls full of the wrath of God,</u> who lives forever and ever. (Revelation 15:7)

Reexamining the Pre-Wrath Rapture

Below are three essential points of the Pre-wrath view.

1. Sixth seal celestial disturbances match Jesus' rapture prerequisites (Revelation 6:12-14, Matthew 24:29-31)

2. Wrath of God starts after the sixth seal is opened (Revelation 6:15-17)

3. Jesus will take raptured believers to His Father's House for at least the last five months of the tribulation. (John 14:1-4)

Sixth seal celestial disturbances match Jesus' rapture prerequisites (Revelation 6:12-14, Matthew 24:29-31)

The first two points were used for the Rapture Fusion. The rapture will take place between the sixth and seventh seals. As the sixth seal is broken, the sky is opened (Revelation 6:14), and those on earth are in the "presence of Him who sits on the throne" (Revelation 6:16). The celestial disturbances match those before the gathering of the elect in the sky in Matthew

24:29-31, and the rapture can be before the wrath mentioned in Revelation 6:16. Thus, the Pre-Wrath name for the system.

While the Pre-Wrath system is Biblical in where it places the rapture, there is a giant elephant in the room; that system alone does not meet the rapture prerequisite of being "at the last trumpet" (1 Corinthians 15:52). That might not be a big deal if there were no trumpets in Revelation, but that of course is not the case. Trumpets play a major role in Revelation, and are elaborated upon in chapters 8-11. Furthermore, the seventh and last trumpet announces "The kingdom of the world has become *the kingdom* of our Lord and of His Christ" (Revelation 11:15). The worship changes from "who is and who was and who is to come" (Revelation 1:4), to "who are and who were," leaving off the "is to come" because He comes at the seventh trumpet. At that last trumpet we are told He has "begun to reign". The seventh trumpet is for believers (at least in part), announcing our King, and therefore the last trumpet. The seventh trumpet passage is clearly a second coming passage, which aligns perfectly with the "last trumpet" resurrection and rapture passage of 1 Corinthians 15:51-52, not to mention the other rapture passages with a trumpet, Matthew 24:29-31, and 1 Thessalonians 4:16-17. Now that we see John's use of the literary style of recapitulation, we can easily fit the puzzle pieces together and see that the seventh trumpet will be blown between the sixth and seventh seals. This is the essence of Rapture Fusion: placing the sixth seal at the end of the seven year tribulation, followed by the seventh trumpet, and the seven bowls of the wrath of God during the seventh seal.

Some speculate that the "last trumpet" (1 Corinthians 15:51-52) will be during Rosh Hashanah, the Feast of Trumpets. That seems like a logical guess, based on other messianic events falling on days of feasts: Jesus died during the feast of Passover, being the Passover Lamb, was buried during the feast of Unleavened Bread, rose at the Feast of First Fruits, and the Holy Spirit came at the feast of Pentecost. Each of the Spring feasts was fulfilled during Jesus' first coming. It is possible His second coming will fulfill the Fall feasts. Jesus may return on the Feast of Trumpets, finish Armageddon on the Festival of Atonement, and dwell with us during the Millennial reign starting on the Feast of Tabernacles. The temple may even be rededicated on Chanukah. But, the guess that He will return on the Feast of Trumpets does not make the "last trumpet" prerequisite go away. If the seven trumpets chronologically follow the seven seals, even if Rosh Hashanah is celebrated between the sixth and seventh seals, the Rosh Hashanah trumpet still would not be the "last trumpet" since it would be followed by seven trumpets. However, if Revelation is not chronological, but instead cyclical, we can speculate that the seventh trumpet will be on Rosh Hashanah between the sixth and seventh seals, and thus fulfilling the "last trumpet" prophesy. The rapture, resurrection, and return of Jesus may not happen on the Feast of Trumpets, but they will happen at the "last trumpet," the seventh trumpet (Revelation 11:15).

Wrath of God starts after the sixth seal is opened (Revelation 6:15-17)

The Pre-Wrath system is partially correct in that the wrath of God starts, after the sixth seal. However, the Pre-Wrath view usually calls the seven trumpets in Revelation the wrath of God. The Bible does not call the seven trumpets wrath. The word "wrath" is first used during the sixth seal (Revelation 6:16-17), but is not used again until after the seventh trumpet (Revelation 11:18). The wrath in Revelation 6:16-17, Revelation 11:18, and the wrath in Revelation 16 are all the same event. They are not the seven trumpet judgments. The words "judgment" or "judge" are not used until after the seventh trumpet either, the same verse as "wrath", Revelation 11:18. Jesus comes down with judgment after the seventh trumpet. The effects of the prior trumpets are not God's wrath or judgments. The sixth trumpet is from four bound angels. Since only fallen angels would be bound, they must be demons, and not God's wrath.

> 14 one saying to the sixth angel who had the trumpet, "Release the <u>four angels who are bound</u> at the great river Euphrates." (Revelation 9:14)

The fifth trumpet is not God's wrath either. The demonic "locusts" from the fifth trumpet are spoken of throughout the Bible (Genesis 6:1-4, Jude 1:6-8, 2 Peter 2:4-5, 1 Peter 3:18-20). The "locust" king is also demonic, being the angel from the abyss.

> 11 They have as king over them, the <u>angel of the abyss</u>; his name in Hebrew is Abaddon, and in the Greek he has the name Apollyon. (Revelation 9:11)

The fourth trumpet also involves demons, as a "third of the stars were struck" (Revelation 8:12).

> 4 And his tail swept away <u>a third of the stars of heaven and threw them to the earth</u>. And the dragon stood before the woman who was about to give birth, so that when she gave birth he might devour her child (Revelation 12:4).

> 9 And the great dragon was thrown down, the serpent of old who is called the devil and Satan, who deceives the whole world; he was thrown

down to the earth, and <u>his angels were thrown down with him</u>. (Revelation 12:9)

One of the effects of the fourth trumpet is not wrath, but for "the sake of the elect" (Matthew 24:22), "the day would not shine for a third of it, and the night in the same way" (Revelation 8:12). Shortening the day and the night by a third, from 24-hour days to 16-hour days, is what Jesus foretold in the Olivet Discourse.

> 22 "Unless those <u>days had been cut short</u>, no life would have been saved; but for the sake of the elect those <u>days will be cut short</u>. (Matthew 24:22)

The number of days of the last half of the tribulation is fixed at 1,260 days and cannot be cut short. However, the length of the days can be cut short by a third, as described in the fourth trumpet.

> 12 The fourth angel sounded, and a third of the sun and a third of the moon and <u>a third of the stars were struck</u>, so that a third of them would be darkened and <u>the day would not shine for a third of it, and the night in the same way</u>. (Revelation 8:12)

The third trumpet is another warning of demonic activity, and not the wrath of God. A demon named Wormwood is described as a star that fell. The "star" later opens the abyss with a key.

> 10 The third angel sounded, and a <u>great star fell from heaven</u>, burning like a torch, and it fell on a third of the rivers and on the springs of waters. 11 The name of the star is called <u>Wormwood</u>; and

a third of the waters became wormwood, and many men died from the waters, because they were made bitter. (Revelation 8:10-11)

1 Then the fifth angel sounded, and I saw a <u>star from heaven which had fallen to the earth; and the key of the bottomless pit was given to him.</u> (Revelation 9:1)

The second trumpet is another demonic warning. "[S]omething like a great mountain burning with fire was thrown" (Revelation 8:8) is similar to Satan being thrown, and fits with the demonic themes of the other trumpets.

9 And <u>the great dragon</u> was <u>thrown</u> down, the serpent of old who is called the devil and Satan, who deceives the whole world; he was <u>thrown</u> down to the earth, and his angels were thrown down with him. (Revelation 12:9)

Finally, the first trumpet is not against humans, and therefore not the wrath of God that 1 Thessalonians 5:9 says believers will be protected from. The first trumpet effects the earth, trees, and grass, and not people directly.

The seven trumpets in Revelation are warnings, not wrath, nor judgments. The first six warn of demonic activity that is about to start. The seventh warns of Jesus, who is coming back with wrath and judgment.

The contents of the scroll with the seven seals are not wrath either. As alluded to in Revelation, please stop for a moment and pray for both you and me to have ears to hear.

> If anyone has an ear, let him hear. (Revelation 13:9)

The contents of the scroll seem so obvious to me. If I am wrong, I would like the Holy Spirit to give me ears to hear the truth. The contents of the scroll are not wrath, not a will, not a plan for the rest of the tribulation, not a title deed to the earth, nor the seven trumpets. Let's take a look at what is said about the scroll. Note, while some translations use the word "book," books as we know them had not been invented by the first century. What John wrote throughout Revelation was "scroll." The scroll was in the "right hand of Him who sat on the throne," namely God the Father. But interestingly enough, not even God the Father was able to open the scroll, "for no one in heaven or on the earth or under the earth was able to open the book or to look into it" (Revelation 5:3). There was only one who could open the scroll, the "Lamb standing, as if slain" (Revelation 5:6). I am guessing when most of us read that a "Lamb standing, as if slain" (Revelation 5:6), "took the book out of the right hand of Him who sat on the throne" (Revelation 5:7), our minds automatically just translate that to "Jesus took the scroll." While that is true, it misses the graphic imagery John is describing. In other words, John described a dead baby sheep who took a scroll from God the Father. Visualize that for a moment. John is using these graphic images to leave an impression on the readers. I think we have sung so many songs about the Lamb that we have become numb to this passage. The Shepherd became the baby Sheep, and He died to obtain this scroll. Notice the worship after the Lamb takes the scroll, "for You were slain, and purchased for God with Your blood *men*" (Revelation 5:9). Taking the scroll is tied to purchasing people.

> 9 And they sang a new song, saying,
> "Worthy are You to take the book and to break its
> seals; for You were slain, and purchased for God
> with Your blood _men_ from every tribe and tongue
> and people and nation. (Revelation 5:9)

Jesus did not purchase wrath. Anyone can purchase wrath. We earn wrath by sinning.

> 23 For the wages of sin is death, but the free gift of
> God is eternal life in Christ Jesus our Lord.
> (Romans 6:23)

God the Father is free to pour out wrath as He chooses. He does not need to slay the Lamb for wrath to be poured out. Furthermore, the scroll is not a will. God the Father is not dying, because He is eternal (Revelation 15:7). He does not need a will. Nor is the scroll a title deed to the earth. Jesus was not slain to purchase the earth. He was slain to redeem mankind, just as the heavenly worship emphasizes, He "purchased for God with [His] blood _men_ from every tribe and tongue and people and nation" (Revelation 5:9). The scroll is not a plan for the rest of the tribulation. There are many end times prophesies in the Old Testament, before the Lamb was slain, which illustrate the plan was known before the Lamb was slain. Finally, the contents of the scroll are not the seven trumpets, the seven bowls, nor the seven thunders. We have seen the need for recapitulation in the previous chapters of this book, for example the need to line up the last trumpet, between the sixth and seventh seals, so the seven trumpets cannot come out of the scroll after the seals are broken.

Let's see if the rest of the Bible can help us understand the contents of the sealed scroll described in Revelation 5. Daniel is told to seal a scroll in Daniel 12.

> 1 "Now at that time Michael, the great prince who stands *guard* over the sons of your people, will arise. And there will be a <u>time of distress such as never occurred</u> since there was a nation until that time; and at that time your people, <u>everyone who is found written in the book, will be rescued</u>.
> 2 "Many of those who <u>sleep in the dust of the ground will awake</u>, these <u>to everlasting life</u>, but the others to disgrace *and* everlasting contempt.
> 3 "Those who have insight will shine brightly like the brightness of the expanse of heaven, and those who lead the many to righteousness, like the stars forever and ever.
> 4 "But as for you, Daniel, conceal these words and <u>seal up the book until the end of time</u>; many will go back and forth, and knowledge will increase."
> (Daniel 12:1-4)

The similarities are striking. Just like the tribulation John is describing in Revelation, Daniel is told of a "time of distress such as never occurred" (Daniel 12:1). In Daniel's scroll, there are names of those who will receive "everlasting life," or more specifically, those who will be resurrected, as "those who sleep in the dust of the ground will awake" (Daniel 12:2). Revelation also speaks of those who will be resurrected and have their name in a scroll.

5 The rest of the dead did not come to life until the thousand years were completed. <u>This is the first resurrection.</u>

12 And I saw <u>the dead,</u> the great and the small, <u>standing</u> before the throne, and books were opened; and <u>another book was opened,</u> which is <u>*the book* of life;</u> and the dead were judged from the things which were written in the books, according to their deeds.

15 And if anyone's <u>name</u> was not found written in the <u>book of life,</u> he was thrown into the lake of fire.(Revelation 20:5, 12, 15)

Daniel sealed a scroll, with names in it. The names were of those who would be resurrected to eternal life after the most distressing time in the earth's history. In Revelation, there is a sealed scroll with names of those who will be resurrected to life after the most distressing time in the earth's history. In case we miss that the sealed scroll that the slain lamb takes is the scroll or "book of life," John ties it all together four us.

8 All who dwell on the earth will worship him, *everyone* whose name has not been written from the foundation of the world in the <u>book of life of the Lamb who has been slain.</u> (Revelation 13:8)

Remember that dead baby Sheep that took the scroll in Revelation 5? Revelation 13:8 also has a dead baby Sheep with a scroll. There are only two passages in the Bible that have a slain Lamb with a scroll, Revelation 5:1-8:1 and Revelation 13:8. The scroll with seven seals that Jesus takes from the Father in Revelation 5 is the scroll of life, or the book of life. It is not a scroll of wrath, but a scroll of life. I think the very next verse after Revelation 13:8 is so divinely placed "If anyone has an ear, let him hear." (Revelation 13:9)

Jesus will take raptured believers to His Father's House for at least the last five months of the tribulation. (John 14:1-4)

> 1 "Do not let your heart be troubled; believe in God, believe also in Me.
> 2 "In My Father's house are many dwelling places; if it were not so, I would have told you; for <u>I go to prepare a place for you</u>.
> 3 "If I go and prepare a place for you, <u>I will come again and receive you to Myself, that where I am, *there* you may be also.</u>
> 4 "And you know the way where I am going."
> (John 14:1-4)

The idea that Jesus will take believers to His Father's house during the tribulation, is not supported by scripture. This passage is not about a Pre-Tribulation, Mid-Tribulation, nor a Pre-Wrath rapture, and not even a Post-Tribulation rapture for that matter. The tribulation is not mentioned. Seven years, three-and-a-half years, or months are not mentioned. The rooms in the Fathers house that Jesus is preparing are in the New Jerusalem, where we will live with Jesus and the Father forever, on the new earth.

> 1 Then I saw a <u>new heaven</u> and a <u>new earth</u>; for the first heaven and the first earth passed away, and there is no longer *any* sea.
> 2 And I saw the holy city, <u>new Jerusalem</u>, coming

down <u>out of heaven from God</u>, made ready as a bride adorned for her husband.

3 And I heard a loud voice from the throne, saying, "Behold, the tabernacle of God is among men, and <u>He will dwell among them</u>, and they shall be His people, and God Himself will be among them, (Revelation 21:1-3)

Jesus is preparing a place for us to live on the new earth after His next coming, not a place for us to live in heaven.

Reexamining the Mid-Tribulation Rapture

Previously I provided seven aspects of the Mid-Tribulation view:

1. Rapture at the seventh trumpet (1 Corinthians 15:51-52, Revelation 11:15-17).

2. Seven trumpets start before the middle of the tribulation (Revelation 8-11).

3. There will be a future seven year tribulation (Daniel 9:27)

4. The rapture will take place in the middle of the tribulation (2 Thessalonians 2:1-4).

5. The rapture will take place before the wrath of God (1 Thessalonians 5:9).

6. Jesus will take raptured believers to His Father's House for the last three and a half years of tribulation. (John 14:1-4).

7. Two resurrections/raptures of believers are needed, one before and one after the last three and a half years of tribulation. (Revelation 20:4).

Let's reexamine each of them.

Rapture at the seventh trumpet (1 Corinthians 15:51-52, Revelation 11:15-17)

This point was used as part of Rapture Fusion. The rapture will take place at the seventh and last trumpet. However, according to scripture the timing of the seventh trumpet is not in the middle of the seven-year tribulation as Mid-Tribulationalists believe. Instead it will be at the end.

Seven trumpets start before the middle of the tribulation (Revelation 8-11)

This point was also used as part of Rapture Fusion. The seven trumpets cover roughly the same time period as the seven seals. For example, the seventh trumpet will be blown between the sixth and seventh seals. The first five trumpets need to be blown before the mid-point of the tribulation, just as the first four seals need to be opened before the mid-point.

There will be a future seven year tribulation (Daniel 9:27)

This point is consistent with the Pre-Tribulation view, and was included in Rapture Fusion. The Mid-Tribulation view focuses on the middle of the seven year tribulation.

The rapture will take place in the middle of the tribulation (2 Thessalonians 2:1-4)

While the middle of Daniel's seventieth seven (the tribulation) is very important (Daniel 9:27, and Matthew 24:15), and the rapture cannot take place before the middle (2 Thessalonians 2:1-4), the rapture will not take place in the middle of the seven year tribulation.

First, "immediately after the tribulation …THEY WILL GATHER TOGETHER His elect" (Matthew 24:29-31). The rapture will be immediately after the tribulation, not in the middle of it. The middle of the tribulation was several verses prior at Matthew 24:15. Second, the sixth seal is after the middle of the tribulation so the rapture would have to be as well. Finally, the first resurrection, which is before or part of the rapture, is after the middle of the seven-year tribulation. Since those resurrected did not take the mark of the beast, which will start to be enforced after the middle of the seven-year tribulation.

> 4 Then I saw thrones, and they sat on them, and judgment was given to them. And I *saw* the souls of those who had been beheaded because of their testimony of Jesus and because of the word of God, and those who had not worshiped the beast or his image, and had not received the mark on their forehead and on their hand; and they came to life and reigned with Christ for a thousand years. (Revelation 20:4)

The rapture will take place before the wrath of God (1 Thessalonians 5:9)

All Pre-Millennial rapture views hold to this doctrine, but define when the wrath starts differently. The Mid-Tribulation view is most similar to the Post-Tribulation view in that both define the seven bowls as the wrath of God. The difference is that the Mid-Tribulation view allows the seven bowls to be poured out throughout the last half of the tribulation while most Post-Tribulation views require the bowls to be poured out only at the very end.

Jesus will take raptured believers to His Father's House for the last three and a half years of tribulation. (John 14:1-4)

See the John 14:1-4 section on page 165 in the "Reexamining the Pre-Wrath Rapture" chapter.

Two resurrections/raptures of believers are needed, one before and one after the last three-and-a-half years of tribulation. (Revelation 20:4)

While the Pre-Tribulation and Mid-Tribulation rapture views require two raptures and two resurrections of believers, that need is not supported by scripture. If one resurrection is before the tribulation, another would be needed after the tribulation for all those who become believers during the tribulation. However, none of the resurrection passages (Matthew 24, Mark 13, John 5, 1 Corinthians 15, 1 Thessalonians 4, 2 Thessalonians 2) mention two resurrections of believers. Revelation 20:6 and John 5:28-29 do indicate there are two resurrections, the first is for believers and the second (the second death) is for unbelievers.

4 Then I saw thrones, and they sat on them, and judgment was given to them. And I *saw* the souls of those who had been beheaded because of their testimony of Jesus and because of the word of God, and those who had not worshiped the beast or his image, and had not received the mark on their forehead and on their hand; and they came to life and reigned with Christ for a thousand years.

5 The rest of the dead did not come to life until the thousand years were completed. This is the first resurrection.

6 Blessed and holy is the one who has a part in the first resurrection; over these the second death has no power, but they will be priests of God and of Christ and will reign with Him for a thousand years. (Revelation 20:4-6)

14 Then death and Hades were thrown into the lake of fire. This is the second death, the lake of fire.

15 And if anyone's name was not found written in the book of life, he was thrown into the lake of fire. (Revelation 20:14-15)

28 "Do not marvel at this; for an hour is coming, in which all who are in the tombs will hear His voice,

29 and will come forth; those who did the good *deeds* to a resurrection of life, those who committed the evil *deeds* to a resurrection of judgment. (John 5:28-29)

The "first resurrection," in Revelation 20, is after beast worship, and before the millennium. There is no indication that the "first resurrection" spans three and a half or more years. The "first resurrection" is at a single point in time, which aligns with every other resurrection passage in the Bible. The same is true of the John 5 passage, where it says there will be "an hour" for "those who did the good *deeds* to [have] a resurrection of life." An hour is clearly not spread over seven years. There is only one resurrection of believers, and it is at the end of the tribulation.

There are no passages in the Bible that mention two raptures. The gathering in the sky (Matthew 24:29-31) that Pre-Tribulationalists and Mid-Tribulationalists would have to call a second rapture, takes place after the tribulation and there is no other mention of a rapture in that passage that takes place before the tribulation.

> 29 "But <u>immediately after the tribulation of those days</u> THE SUN WILL BE DARKENED, AND THE MOON WILL NOT GIVE ITS LIGHT, AND THE STARS WILL FALL from the sky, and the powers of the heavens will be shaken. 30 "And then the sign of the Son of Man will appear in the sky, and then all the tribes of the earth will mourn, and they will see the SON OF MAN COMING ON THE CLOUDS OF THE SKY with power and great glory.
> 31 "And He will send forth His angels with A GREAT TRUMPET and <u>THEY WILL GATHER TOGETHER His elect from the four winds, from one end of the sky to the other</u>. (Matthew 24:29-31)

172

Reexamining the Pre-Tribulation Rapture

Previously, I provided eight aspects of the Pre-Tribulation view:

1. There will be a future seven year tribulation (Daniel 9:27).

2. The rapture will take place before the wrath of God (1 Thessalonians 5:9).

3. The rapture will take place before the seven year tribulation (Revelation 3:10).

4. The word "church" is used in Revelation 1-3, but not Revelation 4-19 (Revelation 1-19).

5. The Rapture takes place at or before Revelation 4:1 (Revelation 4:1).

6. Jesus will take raptured believers to His Father's House for the seven year tribulation. (John 14:1-4).

7. Two resurrections/raptures of believers are needed, one before and one after the seven year tribulation. (Revelation 20:4).

8. The rapture is imminent (Revelation 22:7).

9. Jesus would not allow His Bride to be treated that way (2 Corinthians 11:2).

There will be a future seven year tribulation (Daniel 9:27)

See below.

The rapture will take place before the wrath of God (1 Thessalonians 5:9)

Points 1 and 2 are included in Rapture Fusion. There will be a seven year tribulation, which is also known as Daniel's 70th seven. God will be faithful to His word and rescue believers from the wrath to come. However, the Pre-Tribulation idea that the wrath of God is the entire seven years is not scriptural. The seven bowls are explicitly called the wrath of God. Nothing else in Revelation is called that.

> 1 Then I heard a loud voice from the temple, saying to the seven angels, "Go and pour out on the earth the <u>seven bowls of the wrath of God</u>." (Revelation 16:1)

We can identify when the bowls will be poured out from other sections of Revelation. The bowls (Revelation 16) are poured out after the sixth seal (Revelation 6:12), and after the seventh trumpet (Revelation 11:15).

> 16 and they said to the mountains and to the rocks, "Fall on us and hide us from the presence of Him who sits on the throne, and from <u>the wrath of the Lamb;</u>

17 for the great <u>day of their wrath has come,</u> and who is able to stand?" (Revelation 6:16-17)

18 "And the nations were enraged, and <u>Your wrath</u> came, and the time *came* for the dead to be judged, and *the time* to reward Your bond-servants the prophets and the saints and those who fear Your name, the small and the great, and to destroy those who destroy the earth." (Revelation 11:18)

Using Rapture Fusion, we can see that the seventh trumpet is blown between the sixth and seventh seals, and the seven bowls are poured out between the seventh trumpet and the seventh seal (inclusively). Since the rapture takes place at the seventh trumpet, God is faithful and will rescue believers from the seven bowls of the wrath of God.

There will still be believers on the earth during the seven-year tribulation.

11 And there was given to each of them a white robe; and they were told that they should rest for a little while longer, until *the number of* their fellow servants and their <u>brethren who were to be killed</u> even as they had been, would be completed also. (Revelation 6:11)

17 So the dragon was enraged with the woman, and went off to make war with the rest of her children, <u>who keep the commandments of God and hold to the testimony of Jesus</u>. (Revelation 12:17)

7 It was also given to him to make war with the
saints and to overcome them, and authority over
every tribe and people and tongue and nation was
given to him. (Revelation 13:7)

13 And I heard a voice from heaven, saying,
"Write, 'Blessed are the dead who die in the Lord
from now on!' " "Yes," says the Spirit, "so that
they may rest from their labors, for their deeds
follow with them." (Revelation 14:13)

Pre-Tribulationalist and Mid-Tribulationalists believe those
believers during the tribulation are people that come to Christ
after the rapture. The problem is, why are those tribulation
saints destined for wrath? Didn't Jesus die for those believers
just as much as He died for the believers before the tribulation?

9 For God has not destined us for wrath, but for
obtaining salvation through our Lord Jesus Christ,
10 who died for us, so that whether we are awake
or asleep, we will live together with Him.
11Therefore encourage one another and build up
one another, just as you also are doing. (1
Thessalonians 5:9-11)

What encouragement would there be for those who come to
Christ after the rapture, but before or during the wrath? It does
not make sense that God destined the tribulation saints for
wrath, even though they obtain salvation. This passage, and
others like it, that are so often used to support the Pre-
Tribulation and Mid-Tribulation views actually prove those
views to be false, because if they were true, those saved after
the rapture would be destined for wrath, which clearly

contradicts 1 Thessalonians 5:9-11. No one can come to Christ between the rapture and the wrath of God, otherwise those Jesus died for would be destined for wrath.

The rapture will take place before the seven year tribulation (Revelation 3:10)

There are a few reasons why Revelation 3:10 is improperly interpreted from the Pre-Tribulation perspective. Any one of these reasons prohibits the use of this text as support for the Pre-Tribulation doctrine. First, take a look at the text:

> 10 'Because you have kept the word of My perseverance, I also will <u>keep you from</u> the <u>hour of testing</u>, that *hour* which is about to come upon the whole world, to test those who dwell on the earth. (Revelation 3:10)

1. Revelation chapter one has an introduction. After the introduction, there is a vision of Jesus with seven stars and seven lamp stands. Then, in Revelation 1:19, Jesus says,

   > "Therefore write the <u>things which you have seen</u>, and the <u>things which are</u>, and the <u>things which will take place after these things</u>." (Revelation 1:19)

Jesus was kind enough to give us the start of an outline for Revelation. "The things which you have seen" are the first vision of Jesus, the stars, and the lamp stands. "[T]he things which are," are the things in Revelation that were present in John's day, namely the seven churches, to whom Jesus is dictating letters in chapters 2 and 3 of Revelation. The final section in Jesus' outline is "the things which will take place after these things." Revelation chapters 4-22 are about future things that take place after the things which are. Revelation 3:10 falls in the section of "the things which are." The church of Philadelphia was a real church in the first century. There was a letter written to it, which included "I also will keep you from the hour of testing" (Revelation 3:10). However, that was a message specifically for the first century church of Philadelphia, which is included in "the things that are." This is not in the section "the things which will take place after these things," Revelation 3:10, is not a prophesy for the future global church thousands of years later.

2. The Greek phrase "tereo ek" is only found in two passages. Once in Revelation 3:10, which the NASB translates as "keep you from," and the other in John 17:15 translated "keep them from." Both were Jesus' words recorded by John, so the Greek should be consistent. John and Jesus were kind enough to explain in John 17:15 that "keep them from" does not mean "take them out," as Pre-Tribulationists would have you believe about Revelation 3:10. It just means they will be protected from a trial, while remaining on earth, and not taken out of the trial.

> Because you have kept My command to persevere, I also will <u>keep you from</u> [tereo ek] the hour of trial which shall come upon the whole world, to test those who dwell on the earth (Revelation 3:10)

> <u>I do not pray that You should take them out of the world</u>, but that You should <u>keep them from</u> [tereo ek] the evil one. (John 17:15)

3. The promise to the church of Philadelphia in Revelation 3:10 was only in reference to "the hour of testing". Times are

very important in Revelation. An hour is not seven years. Even if it is not a literal hour, it needs to be viewed as a shorter amount of time than say, "one thousand two hundred and sixty days" (Revelation 12:6b), which is half the tribulation (3.5 years). Revelation 3:10 is not about keeping a church from seven years of testing. Jesus clearly said this promise is for "the hour of testing." This passage does more to disprove the Pre-Tribulation, Mid-Tribulation, and Pre-Wrath rapture positions than it does to prove them, because those views require the church to be gone for more than an hour.

I presented three reasons why Revelation 3:10 is not describing a Pre-Tribulation rapture. The first, it is in the section "the things which are" so it is not about a far future hour of trial. The second, "keep you from" does not mean "take them out of the world." And finally, it is about an "hour of trial" not seven years of trial. Choose your favorite of the three reasons why Revelation 3:10 does not support a Pre-Tribulation rapture, because any one of the three should be sufficient to remove this passage from the Pre-Tribulation rapture debate.

The word "church" is used in Revelation 1-3, but not Revelation 4-19 (Revelation 1-19)

While it is an interesting fact that the words "church" or "churches" is found 19 times in Revelation 1-3 and 0 times in Revelation 4-19, we should not base our doctrine on what is omitted. Using the omission argument, as Pre-Tribulationalists often do, that the absence of the word "church" means the church was raptured from the earth, could equally be used to prove the church was not raptured into heaven. Much of Revelation 4-19 takes place in heaven and the church is never mentioned. We should base our doctrine on what **is** said. The most clear rapture passage in Revelation is in chapter 14:14-16:

> 14 Then I looked, and behold, a <u>white cloud</u>, and sitting on the cloud *was* one like a <u>son of man</u>, having a golden <u>crown</u> on His head and a sharp sickle in His hand.
> 15 And another angel came out of the temple, crying out with a loud voice to Him who sat on the cloud, "Put in your sickle and reap, for the hour to reap has come, because the <u>harvest of the earth is ripe</u>."
> 16 Then <u>He</u> who sat on the <u>cloud</u> swung His sickle over the earth, and <u>the earth was reaped</u>.
> (Revelation 14:14-16)

The most clear resurrection passage is in Revelation 20:4-6:

> 4 Then I saw thrones, and they sat on them, and judgment was given to them. And I *saw* the <u>souls</u> of those who had been beheaded because of their testimony of Jesus and because of the word of God, and those who had not worshiped the beast or his image, and had not received the mark on their forehead and on their hand; and they <u>came to life and reigned with Christ for a thousand years</u>.
> 5 The rest of the dead did not come to life until the thousand years were completed. <u>This is the first resurrection</u>.
> 6 Blessed and holy is the one who has a part in the <u>first resurrection</u>; over these the second death has no power, but they will be priests of God and of

> Christ and will reign with Him for a thousand
> years. (Revelation 20:4-6)

Neither of these clear rapture and resurrection passages are before the tribulation. It makes far better logic to base a doctrine on what is clearly conveyed, as opposed to on a word that is not present.

One[3] can do a fascinating word study on the words "church" or "churches" in Revelation. Of the 20 uses of the word "church" in Revelation, 19 of them are in red letters. This means Jesus used the word "church" or "churches" 19 times, and John used the word "churches" once (Revelation 1:4) in all of Revelation. There are only red letters in four chapters of Revelation, chapters 1-3 and chapter 22, and the word "church" is only used in the same four chapters. Since John used the word one time, that does not make it a pattern. We do not see John habitually using the word "church," and then abruptly stopping. We see John using the word "church" once in the introduction.

> 4 John to the seven churches that are in Asia:
> Grace to you and peace, from Him who is and
> who was and who is to come, and from the seven
> Spirits who are before His throne, (Revelation 1:4)

Jesus used the word "church" consistently when He spoke in Revelation. One speaker used the word "church" often, and the other did not. That does not mean the church was not on earth in the latter speaker's sections. John simply used other words when describing the church (e.g. "saints" in Revelation 5:8, 8:3-4, 11:18, 13:7-10, 14:12, 16:6, 17:6, 18:20-24, 19:8, 20:9). The use of,

---

3 Dave Bussard http://thepre-wrathtribune.blogspot.com/2007/06/church-in-revelation.html

or lack of, the word "church" in Revelation is not a sound defense for a belief system about where the church resides.

The Rapture takes place at or before Revelation 4:1 (Revelation 4:1)

While John's spirit went up to Heaven in Revelation 4:1-2, it does not mean the church will be raptured and resurrected before the tribulation.

> 1 After these things I looked, and behold, a door *standing* open in heaven, and the first voice which I had heard, like *the sound* of a trumpet speaking with me, said, "Come up here, and I will show you what must take place after these things."
> 2 Immediately I was in the Spirit; and behold, a throne was standing in heaven, and One sitting on the throne. (Revelation 4:1-2)

John's spirit went up to Heaven in the first century to learn "the things which will take place after these things" (Revelation 1:19c). John did not represent all believers when he alone went up. There is no indication in Revelation 4:1, or in the prior outlined passage, "the things which are" (Revelation 1:19b), that a Pre-Tribulation rapture of the church occurs.

Jesus will take raptured believers to His Father's House for the seven year tribulation. (John 14:1-4)

See the John 14:1-4 section on page 165 in the "Reexamining the Pre-Wrath Rapture" chapter.

Two resurrections/raptures of believers are needed, one before and one after the seven year tribulation. (Revelation 20:4)

See the Revelation 20:4 section on page 170 in the "Reexamining the Mid-Tribulation Rapture" chapter.

The rapture is imminent (Revelation 22:7)

The "imminence of the rapture" is the belief that the rapture can happen at any moment, and that there are no further prophesies that need to be fulfilled before the resurrection and rapture of believers. It is easy to prove there are prophesied events that need to take place before the rapture. Take 1 Corinthians 15:51-52 for example:

> 51 Behold, I tell you a mystery; we will not all sleep, but <u>we will all be changed</u>,
> 52 in a moment, in the twinkling of an eye, at the <u>last trumpet</u>; for the <u>trumpet</u> will sound, and the <u>dead will be raised imperishable</u>, and <u>we will be changed</u>. (1 Corinthians 15:51-52)

There are several events described that must precede the rapture, when those alive "will be changed." First, immediately before the change/rapture, the dead will be raised. Second, before the dead are raised, there will be a "last trumpet." Third, by definition, if there is a last trumpet, there must be a first trumpet. From these two verses alone we can prove there are at least three events that precede the rapture: the first trumpet, the last trumpet, and the resurrection, thus disproving the notion of an imminent rapture. The next chapter, Rapture Prerequisites, will show several additional reasons why the rapture is not imminent.

There are no verses that say the rapture is imminent. The closest scripture comes to suggesting imminence is the warning that Jesus is "coming quickly." But what did Jesus mean by saying He is "coming quickly?"

> 7 "And behold, <u>I am coming quickly</u>. Blessed is he who heeds the words of the prophecy of this book." (Revelation 22:7)

Peter told us,

> 8 But do not let this one *fact* escape your notice, beloved, that with the Lord one day is like a thousand years, and <u>a thousand years like one day</u>. (2 Peter 3:8)

If the Lord should tarry for 2,000 years after His ascension, for Him that is similar to two days, just a weekend. Coming back after a weekend is pretty quick. Even if He should tarry 7,000 years, for Him that would only be a week, and a fairly quick return.

Also, related to the imminence argument, is that the Lord is going to come like a thief in the night. The idea is that Jesus is going to rapture the believers at any moment, just like a thief can come at any moment.

> 2 For you yourselves know full well that the day of the Lord will come just <u>like a thief in the night</u>. (1 Thessalonians 5:2)

While the idea is based on the Bible, it is a good example of taking a passage out of context. If we continue reading,

4 But you, <u>brethren</u>, are <u>not</u> in darkness, that the day would overtake you <u>like a thief</u>;
5 for you are all sons of light and sons of day. We are not of night nor of darkness;
6 so then let us not sleep as others do, but let us <u>be alert</u> and sober. (1 Thessalonians 5:4-6)

We see Jesus does not come like a thief in the night for the brethren, because we are to be alert. He comes like a thief for those in darkness. 1 Thessalonians 5 does not teach the imminence of the rapture, rather it encourages the brethren to be alert and looking for the signs of His coming.

Jesus would not allow His Bride to be treated that way (2 Corinthians 11:2)

There are no passages that use the phrase, "Bride of Christ." For as much as this phrase gets thrown around in Christian circles, one would think it would be in at least one verse. The closest we get is "betrothed" or "wife:"

> For I am jealous for you with a godly jealousy; for I <u>betrothed</u> you to one husband, so that to <u>Christ</u> I might present you *as* a pure virgin. (2 Corinthians 11:2)

> FOR THIS REASON A MAN SHALL LEAVE HIS FATHER AND MOTHER AND SHALL BE JOINED TO HIS <u>WIFE</u>, AND THE TWO SHALL BECOME ONE FLESH.
> 32 This mystery is great; but I am speaking with reference to <u>Christ and the church</u>. (Ephesians 5:31-32)

Not having the exact wording, "Bride of Christ," is not a big deal because the idea is still there. I would hope most people realize it is an analogy and not to be taken literally. Jesus is not going to literally marry multitudes of Christians from the last two thousand years. He is not literally going to "become one flesh" with anyone or anything. Furthermore, His bride is not limited to the Church. Throughout the Old Testament, Israel plays the role of the wife of God. The most clear example is the entire book of Hosea. One excerpt from Hosea about Israel being the Lord's wife is found in Hosea 2:16.

> 16 When that day comes," says the LORD,
> "you will call me 'my husband'
> instead of 'my master.' (Hosea 2:16 NLT)

Isaiah also refers to Israel as the Lord's wife:

> 4 It will no longer be said to you, "Forsaken,"
> Nor to your land will it any longer be said,
> "Desolate";
> But you will be called, "My delight is in her,"
> And your land, "Married";
> For the LORD delights in you,
> And to Him your land will be married. (Isaiah 62:4)

In some of Jesus' parables, believers are the dinner guests to God's wedding feast (not the bride). In another parable, believers are the bridesmaids.

> 10"Those slaves went out into the streets and gathered together all they found, both evil and good; and the wedding hall was filled with dinner guests. (Matthew 22:10)

186

1 "Then the kingdom of heaven will be comparable to ten virgins, who took their lamps and went out to meet the bridegroom. (Matthew 25:1)

In Revelation, the "Bride of Christ" is the New Jerusalem:

9 Then one of the seven angels who had the seven bowls full of the seven last plagues came and spoke with me, saying, "Come here, I will show you the bride, the wife of the Lamb." And he carried me away in the Spirit to a great and high mountain, and showed me the holy city, Jerusalem, coming down out of heaven from God, (Revelation 21:9-10)

All of that to say, don't take analogies too literally, as they are just a word picture used to convey an idea. God's bride in the Old Testament was treated poorly many times with His approval. They were slaves in Egypt, and captives in Assyria, and Babylon. Jesus' 11 best friends, the foundations of the church, were all martyred, but one. Some of the most godly men and women throughout church history have been tortured and martyred. Even today, Christians all over the world, the "Bride of Christ," are being persecuted. God allows "bad things" to happen to His "Bride" often. These examples prove that when tribulation happens, God allows His people to suffer. Being a "bride" is not going to get either Israel nor the church out of the seven year tribulation.

Part V:
Conclusion

Rapture Prerequisites

According to the Bible there are several events that must take place before the rapture, which are not all accounted for by the traditional Pre-Tribulation, Mid-Tribulation, Pre-Wrath, and Post-Tribulation rapture views.

Rapture Prerequisites:

1. After the Abomination of Desolation.
2. After the tribulation.
3. When the sun and moon are darkened.
4. At the last trumpet.

After the Abomination of Desolation

First, the rapture cannot happen until after the Abomination of Desolation, which takes place three and a half years into Daniel's 70th seven. To help me remember, I have a little saying, "Go to (2) Thessalonians to (2) refute the Pre-Tribulation rapture". Let's look at 2 Thessalonians 2:1-12.

1 Now we request you, brethren, with regard to the <u>coming of our Lord Jesus Christ and our gathering together to Him,</u> (2 Thessalonians 2:1)

The gathering to Him is the rapture. Paul is telling us this passage is about the second coming and the rapture.

2 that you not be quickly shaken from your composure or be disturbed either by a spirit or a message or a letter as if from us, to the effect that <u>the day of the Lord has come.</u> (2 Thessalonians 2:2)

The Day of the Lord is part of the same event as the coming and the gathering. The Day of the Lord starts after the sun and moon are darkened (Joel 2:31). Jesus returns when the sun and moon are darkened (Zechariah 14:4-6), and the elect are gathered in the sky when the sun and moon are darkened (Matthew 24:29-31).

31 "The <u>sun</u> will be turned into <u>darkness</u>
And the <u>moon</u> into <u>blood</u>
<u>Before the</u> great and awesome <u>day of the</u> Lord
comes. (Joel 2:31)

4 In that day <u>His feet will stand on the Mount of Olives,</u> which is in front of Jerusalem on the east; and the Mount of Olives will be split in its middle from east to west by a very large valley, so that half of the mountain will move toward the north and the other half toward the south.
5 You will flee by the valley of My mountains, for the valley of the mountains will reach to Azel; yes, you will flee just as you fled before the earthquake

in the days of Uzziah king of Judah. Then the
LORD, my God, will come, *and* all the holy ones
with Him!
6 In that day there will be no light; the luminaries
will dwindle. (Zechariah 14:4-6)

29 "But immediately after the tribulation of those
days THE SUN WILL BE DARKENED, AND THE MOON WILL
NOT GIVE ITS LIGHT, AND THE STARS WILL FALL from the
sky, and the powers of the heavens will be shaken.
30 "And then the sign of the Son of Man will
appear in the sky, and then all the tribes of the
earth will mourn, and they will see the SON OF
MAN COMING ON THE CLOUDS OF THE SKY with power
and great glory.
31 "And He will send forth His angels with A
GREAT TRUMPET and THEY WILL GATHER TOGETHER His
elect from the four winds, from one end of the sky
to the other. (Matthew 24:29-31)

Now let's continue on in 2 Thessalonians 2.

3 Let no one in any way deceive you, (2
Thessalonians 2:3a)

This is very important, Jesus told us not to be deceived many
times when teaching on the end times, and Paul also warns us
not to be deceived.

for *it will not come* unless the apostasy comes first,
and the man of lawlessness is revealed, the son of
destruction, (2 Thessalonians 2:3b)

The coming of Christ, the rapture, and the Day of the Lord, cannot come until after the man of lawlessness, the son of destruction is revealed. This is talking about the man we call the Antichrist.

> 4 who opposes and exalts himself above every so-called god or object of worship, so that <u>he takes his seat in the temple of God, displaying himself as being God.</u> (2 Thessalonians 2:4)

The rapture cannot take place until after the middle of the tribulation. This passage, in and of itself, disproves the pre-tribulation rapture. Do not be deceived and think that the rapture could take place before the Antichrist is revealed and takes his seat in the temple of God.

> 5 Do you not remember that while I was still with you, I was telling you these things?
> 6 And you know <u>what restrains him now</u>, so that in his time he will be revealed.
> 7 For the mystery of lawlessness is already at work; only <u>he who now restrains *will do so* until he is taken out of the way</u>.
> 8 Then that lawless one will be revealed whom the Lord will slay with the breath of His mouth and bring to an end by the appearance of <u>His coming</u>;
> 9 *that is,* the one whose coming is in accord with the activity of Satan, with all power and signs and false wonders,
> 10 and with all the deception of wickedness for those who perish, because they did not receive the love of the truth so as to be saved.
> 11 For this reason <u>God will send upon them a</u>

deluding influence so that they will believe what
is false,
12 in order that they all may be judged who did
not believe the truth, but took pleasure in
wickedness. (2 Thessalonians 2:5-12)

Just a quick note on verse 7. Some say, "he who now restrains"
is either the church, or the Holy Spirit working through the
church, and that when the church is raptured, the Antichrist
will be unrestrained. Remember, it does not say who the
restrainer is, so we can only guess. We should not base our
rapture theory on a guess, especially when that theory
contradicts clear scripture. My guess is the restrainer is Jesus
who has the key to Hades. When He gives the key to
Wormwood (who empowers the False Prophet), Apollyon (who
empowers the Antichrist) will no longer be restrained.

18 and the living One; and I was dead, and
behold, I am alive forevermore, and I have the
keys of death and of Hades. (Revelation 1:18)

10 The third angel sounded, and a great star fell
from heaven, burning like a torch, and it fell on a
third of the rivers and on the springs of waters.
11 The name of the star is called Wormwood; and
a third of the waters became wormwood, and
many men died from the waters, because they
were made bitter. (Revelation 8:10-11)

1 Then the fifth angel sounded, and I saw a star
from heaven which had fallen to the earth; and the
key of the bottomless pit was given to him
(Revelation 9:1)

11 They have as <u>king</u> over them, <u>the angel of the abyss</u>; his name in Hebrew is Abaddon, and in the Greek he has the name <u>Apollyon</u>. (Revelation 9:11)

After the tribulation

The second prerequisite, which the Pre-Tribulation and Mid-Tribulation rapture views do not meet, is that the rapture occurs after the tribulation. Remember, "pre" means before, and "mid" means middle, so Pre-Tribulationalists believe the rapture is before the tribulation, which is a stark contradiction to scripture.

29 "But immediately <u>after the tribulation</u> of those days THE SUN WILL BE DARKENED, AND THE MOON WILL NOT GIVE ITS LIGHT, AND THE STARS WILL FALL from the sky, and the powers of the heavens will be shaken. 30 "And then the sign of the Son of Man will appear in the sky, and then all the tribes of the earth will mourn, and they will see the <u>SON OF MAN COMING ON THE CLOUDS</u> OF THE SKY with power and great glory.
31 "And He will send forth His angels with <u>A GREAT TRUMPET</u> and <u>THEY WILL GATHER TOGETHER His elect</u> from the four winds, <u>from one end of the sky to the other</u>. (Matthew 24:29-31)

After the tribulation, the angels will gather the elect in the sky. Christ was talking to the foundations of the church, the Apostles, the week He died. He told them the rapture will occur after the tribulation. Mark records it as well.

24 "But in those days, <u>after that tribulation</u>, THE SUN WILL BE DARKENED AND THE MOON WILL NOT GIVE

ITS LIGHT,

25 AND THE STARS WILL BE FALLING from heaven, and the powers that are in the heavens will be shaken.
26 "Then they will see THE SON OF MAN COMING IN CLOUDS with great power and glory.
27 "And then He will send forth the angels, and will gather together His elect from the four winds, from the farthest end of the earth to the farthest end of heaven. (Mark 13:24-27)

Jesus, through Mark, goes on to tell us that the gathering in the sky is not just for the Apostles, or just Jewish people. It is for all believers. It is the gathering of all His elect.

37 "What I say to you I say to all, 'Be on the alert!' " (Mark 13:37)

There is some debate on who the word "elect" is referring to in Matthew 24:31 (above) and Mark 13:27 (above). Does elect mean Jews or believers in Jesus Christ (both Jew and gentile)? "Elect" is an ambiguous term that means chosen. The word is used to refer to Jesus (Luke 23:35), angels (1 Timothy 5:20), individuals (Romans 16:13), and both Jews and Greeks who have been renewed by Christ (Colossians 3:10-12). The question is, who was Jesus referring to as "elect" in Matthew 24:31? The meaning cannot be decisively concluded based on the immediate context. But, when you look at what happens in Matthew 24:29-31 (above), and compare it with other scripture passages, the meaning of elect in this context becomes obvious. The passage includes "SON OF MAN COMING ON THE CLOUDS," "A GREAT TRUMPET," and a gathering in the "sky." In 1 Thessalonians 4:15-17 we see those same elements, "the coming of the Lord," "clouds," "the trumpet of God," and a gathering in the "air."

Therefore, we can conclude the "elect" in Matthew 24:31 are those who will "always be with the Lord," believers in Jesus Christ, both Jew and Gentile. One could come to the same conclusion based on 1 Corinthians 15:51-52.

> 15 For this we say to you by the word of the Lord, that we who are alive and remain until <u>the coming of the Lord</u>, will not precede those who have fallen asleep.
> 16 For <u>the Lord Himself will descend from heaven</u> with a shout, with the voice of *the* archangel and with <u>the</u> <u>trumpet of God</u>, and the dead in Christ will rise first.
> 17 Then we who are alive and remain will be caught up together with them in the <u>clouds</u> to meet the <u>Lord</u> in the <u>air</u>, and so <u>we shall always be with the Lord</u>. (1 Thessalonians 4:15-17)

When Jesus described the end time events in Matthew 24 and Mark 13, He only spoke of one gathering, which was after the tribulation. Jesus did not teach a Pre-Tribulation rapture. He explicitly taught the opposite, a rapture "immediately after the tribulation."

When the sun and moon are darkened

The third requirement that the Pre-Tribulation, Mid-Tribulation, and Post-Tribulation rapture systems do not meet, is that the rapture will occur when the sun and moon are darkened. From the same prior passages:

> 29 "But immediately after the tribulation of those days THE SUN WILL BE DARKENED, AND THE MOON WILL NOT GIVE ITS LIGHT, AND THE STARS WILL FALL from the

sky, and the powers of the heavens will be shaken.
30 "And then the sign of the Son of Man will
appear in the sky, and then all the tribes of the
earth will mourn, and they will see the SON OF
MAN COMING ON THE CLOUDS OF THE SKY with power
and great glory.
31 "And He will send forth His angels with A
GREAT TRUMPET and THEY WILL GATHER TOGETHER His
elect from the four winds, from one end of the sky
to the other. (Matthew 24:29-31)

The sun and moon are darkened and the stars fall after the
Abomination of Desolation. This is the middle of the tribulation
that Jesus described a few verses earlier in Matthew 24:15. The
sixth seal, in Revelation also has sun and moon darkened and
stars falling, and is therefore also after the middle of the
tribulation.

12 I looked when He broke the sixth seal, and
there was a great earthquake; and the sun became
black as sackcloth *made* of hair, and the whole
moon became like blood;
13 and the stars of the sky fell to the earth, as a fig
tree casts its unripe figs when shaken by a great
wind. (Revelation 6:12-14)

The rapture has to happen when the sixth seal is broken. The
Pre-Tribulation rapture, Mid-Tribulation rapture, and Post-
Tribulation rapture do not meet these prerequisites for the
rapture. The Pre-Trib and Mid-Trib views would place the
rapture long before the sixth seal. Most Post-Tribulation
positions place the rapture at least five months (Revelation 9:5)

after the sixth seal (Revelation 6:12-17) and the celestial signs in Matthew 24:29, which would contradict the Matthew passage.

While the Pre-Wrath view does place the rapture when the sun and moon are darkened, it does **not** place Jesus return to earth when the sun and moon are darkened. That does not fit with other scripture. The traditional Pre-Wrath view places the seven trumpets, the seven bowls, and the return of Christ after the rapture, when the sun and moon are darkened. In Zechariah 14:4-6, we are told that the return of Christ to earth also happens when the sun and moon are darkened.

> 4 In that day His feet will stand on the Mount of Olives, which is in front of Jerusalem on the east; and the Mount of Olives will be split in its middle from east to west by a very large valley, so that half of the mountain will move toward the north and the other half toward the south.
> 5 You will flee by the valley of My mountains, for the valley of the mountains will reach to Azel; yes, you will flee just as you fled before the earthquake in the days of Uzziah king of Judah. Then the LORD, my God, will come, *and* all the holy ones with Him!
> 6 In that day there will be no light; the luminaries will dwindle. (Zechariah 14:4-6)

To conclude, the Pre-Tribulation Mid-Tribulation, and Post-Tribulation rapture systems do not place the rapture during the celestial disturbances, in spite of Matthew 24:29-31. Also, none of the four traditional Pre-millennial rapture views place the return of Christ during the celestial disturbances, in spite of Zechariah 14:4-6.

At the last trumpet

The Pre-Tribulation and Pre-Wrath raptures do not meet the last trumpet requirement. There is a trumpet during the rapture.

> 31 "And He will send forth His angels with A GREAT TRUMPET and THEY WILL GATHER TOGETHER His elect from the four winds, from one end of the sky to the other. (Matthew 24:31)

> 16 For the Lord Himself will descend from heaven with a shout, with the voice of *the* archangel and with the trumpet of God, and the dead in Christ will rise first.
> 17 Then we who are alive and remain will be caught up together with them in the clouds to meet the Lord in the air, and so we shall always be with the Lord. (1 Thessalonians 4:16-17)

> 52 in a moment, in the twinkling of an eye, at the last trumpet; for the trumpet will sound, and the dead will be raised imperishable, and we will be changed. (1 Corinthians 15:52)

1 Corinthians 15:52 tells us specifically that the rapture is at the last trumpet. The last trumpet will be the seventh trumpet of Revelation. Not coincidentally, it marks the coming of Christ's kingdom.

> 15 Then the seventh angel sounded; and there were loud voices in heaven, saying,
> "The kingdom of the world has become *the kingdom* of our Lord and of His Christ; and He will reign forever and ever." (Revelation 11:15)

There cannot be another trumpet after the last. 1 Thessalonians 4:16 specifically tells us the trumpet is "the trumpet of God." The seventh trumpet meets this description because the trumpet is blown by the angel from God.

> 2 And I saw the seven angels who stand before God, and seven trumpets were given to them. (Revelation 8:2)

Rapture Prerequisites Conclusion

The four prerequisites presented, and their Biblical support, should completely disprove the four traditional rapture theories. Jesus has to come and rapture the church after the abomination of desolation, after the tribulation, when the sun and moon are darkened, and specifically at the last trumpet. Only Rapture Fusion meets all of the prerequisites.

	After the Abomination of Desolation (2 Thess. 2:4)	After the tribulation (Matt. 24:29-31)	When the sun and moon are darkened (Matt. 24:29-31)	At the last trumpet (1 Cor. 15:52)
Pre-Trib				
Mid-Trib	✓			✓
Pre-Wrath	✓	✓	✓	
Post-Trib	✓	✓		✓
Rapture Fusion	✓	✓	✓	✓

Summary

Rapture Fusion takes the best (most supported by scripture) end times theories from each of the four Pre-Millennial rapture views and merges them together using recapitulation. We have seen from scripture that the rapture cannot take place before the tribulation, as the Pre-Tribulation view requires. Nor can the rapture take place in the middle of the tribulation as the Mid-Tribulation view requires. Rather, according to scripture, the rapture will take place after the tribulation (Matthew 24:29-31), and between the sixth (Revelation 6:12-17) and seventh seals (Revelation 8:1). Between those two seals, the seventh (Revelation 11:15-17) and last trumpet (1 Corinthians 15:51-52) will be blown, before the bowls filled with the wrath of God (Revelation 6:16-17, 11:18, 16) are poured out. Therefore, Rapture Fusion effectively merges the Pre-Wrath and Post-Tribulation rapture views using recapitulation.

I pray this book helps you understand the Revelation of Jesus Christ. That by seeing how extremely cyclical Revelation is, you will better grasp every aspect of Revelation with the help of the Holy Spirit. Remember to ask Him, each time you open the scriptures, to give you ears to hear what the Spirit says. We can clearly see in Revelation that our God wins, but first there will be tribulation that believers will need to overcome. This is the bitter-sweet paradox John was instructed to share.

> 10 I took the little book out of the angel's hand and ate it, and in my mouth it was <u>sweet</u> as honey; and when I had eaten it, my stomach was made <u>bitter</u>. 11 And they said to me, "<u>You must prophesy again</u> concerning many peoples and nations and tongues and kings." (Revelation 10:10-11)

The next logical question is, how do we prepare for the coming tribulation? My first thoughts were about stock piling supplies and waiting it out in a bunker. While preparing for disasters is a good thing, I could not imagine Jesus saying, "Well done my good and faithful servant, you did a good job hiding in the ground." Instead, we need to prepare to use our "talents" to reap where our Master did not sow (Matthew 25:14-30). We need to prepare by memorizing scripture for a time when Bibles and Bible software may be illegal. We need to prepare mentally to not take the mark of the beast. Without the mark, people will not be able to buy or sell (Revelation 13:17). That means we will probably have to go hungry. We may have to watch our kids or our grand-kids starve to death, because we chose not to get the mark of the beast. Now is the time to mentally prepare for that possibility. When is the best time to decide not to have premarital sex, before you have a significant other, or when you are alone with a significant other? One would be much more likely to successfully resist temptation having decided long beforehand. Similarly, we need to firmly decide not to take the mark, before we get hungry. We also need to prepare the church. Paul warns believers to not be deceived concerning the rapture and the coming of Jesus on the day of the Lord:

> 3 Let no one in any way deceive you, for *it will not come* unless the apostasy comes first, and the man of lawlessness is revealed, the son of destruction, (2 Thessalonians 2:3)

We need to tell those in the church what the Bible teaches about the tribulation. Some will be deceived and there will be an apostasy before Jesus comes back. "Apostasy" means a falling away from the faith. Jesus said:

> 10 "At that time many will fall away and will betray one another and hate one another. (Matthew 24:10)

Rapture views that teach that the church will not be here for the tribulation, or be pressured to take the mark of the beast, are dangerous. There will be church-goers who will not recognize the tribulation, or will be tricked by the miracles of false Christs.

> 24 "For false Christs and false prophets will arise and will show great signs and wonders, so as to mislead, if possible, even the elect. (Matthew 24:24)

We need to promote sound doctrine in regard to the tribulation and rapture, so that those we minister to will not fall away. Finally, once more, I want to give you the opportunity to believe in Jesus Christ, if you do not already. If you do not believe, the rapture that Christians look forward to means nothing but loss and torment for you. I will conclude with one of my favorite verses. You probably have heard or read it before, but please take your time to let each word sink in. The verse speaks for itself.

> **16** "For God so loved the world, that He gave His only begotten Son, that whoever <u>believes</u> in Him shall not perish, but have eternal life. (John 3:16)

Glossary

A-Millennial	Belief that the millennium is realized now. That the 1,000 years in Revelation 20:1-10 is not a literal 1,000 years, but just a really long time, the entire church age.
Abaddon	Translated from Hebrew it means Destroyer. The Greek translation is Apollyon. Is the [fallen] angelic king of the abyss (Revelation 9:11) who is released to torment those who are not the 144,000 (Revelation 9:4). Most likely, this demonic king named Destroyer will empower the Antichrist who is called the son of destruction (2 Thessalonians 2:3).
Abomination of Desolation	The middle of the seven-year tribulation. When the Antichrist will desecrate the Temple (Daniel 9:27, Daniel 11:31, Matthew 24:15, Mark 13:14, Luke 21:20, 2 Thessalonians 2:4).

Antichrist	This word is found exclusively in 1 John and 2 John (e.g. 1 John 2:18). According to John there have been many antichrists starting from the first century. Other names for the future Antichrist are: Little Horn, Prince, Ruler, False Christ, Man of Lawlessness, Son of Destruction, The Beast, the Beast from the Abyss, The Beast from the Sea. The Antichrist is most likely empowered by the demon Apollyon/Abaddon (Revelation 9:11).
Apollyon	Translated from Greek it means Destroyer. The Hebrew translation is Abaddon. Is the [fallen] angelic king of the abyss (Revelation 9:11) who is released to torment those who are not the 144,000 (Revelation 9:4). Most likely, this demonic king named Destroyer will empower the Antichrist who is called the son of destruction (2 Thessalonians 2:3).

Apostasy	A falling away from the faith. Before Jesus comes back there will be a falling away (2 Thessalonians 2:4).
Beast, The	Usually in reference to the beast from the sea or abyss (Revelation 13:1-10). The Beast is thought to be the Antichrist. However, there is another beast from the earth, said to be the false prophet (Revelation 11:7, Revelation 13:11-18).
Book of Life	Could also be translated Scroll of Life. Written at the foundation of the world (Revelation 13:8). Purchased with the Jesus' blood (Revelation 5:9). Read at the Great White Throne judgment (Revelation 20:12). Contains the names of those who have eternal life (Revelation 20:15).
Bowls	Vials that contained the wrath of God, that will be poured out at the end.
Celestial Disturbances	The darkening of the Sun and Moon, and falling stars before the Day of the Lord (Joel 2:31, Matthew 24:29-31, Revelation 6:12-17).

Classic Pre-Millennialist	Another name for a Post-Trib Pre-Millennialist. The Classic Pre-Millennialist holds to what has been historically the Pre-Millennialist view.
Day of the Lord	Starts when the sixth seal is opened (Revelation 6:12-17), when the sun is darkened and the moon turns to blood (Joel 2:31). It is the coming of the Lord (Matthew 24:29-31). It will be great for some, and terrible for others (Malachi 4:5).
Demons	Fallen angels.
Elect	Means chosen ones. The word is used to refer to Jesus (Luke 23:35), angels (1 Timothy 5:20), individuals (Romans 16:13), and both Jews and Greeks who have been renewed by Christ (Colossians 3:10-12).
Eschatology	The study of the end times.
False Christs	Jesus warned at the end of the age there will be false Christs to "mislead, if possible, even the elect" (Matthew 24:24)

False Prophet	Jesus warned at the end of the age there will be false prophets to "mislead, if possible, even the elect" (Matthew 24:24). The beast from the earth is the False Prophet (Revelation 16:13). The False Prophet is most likely empowered by the demon Wormwood (Revelation 8:11).
Futurist	View that most of Revelation (usually Revelation 4-22) is in the future.
Great Tribulation	Often used for the entire seven year tribulation, but may only be the latter half of the seven year tribulation (Matthew 24:21, Revelation 7:14).
Hades	The Greek equivalent of the Hebrew term sheol, which means neither Heaven nor Hell, rather the grave.
Historicist	View that Revelation is always applicable, throughout the church age. Such that the characters in Revelation are always present in the church age. This causes characters and times to be taken very symbolically.

Historic Pre-Millennialist	Another name for a Post-Trib Pre-Millennialist. Not to be confused with a Historicist. The Historic Pre-Millennialist holds to what has been historically the Pre-Millennialist view.
Idealist	View that Revelation should be read as a parable, as a story to teach a specific lesson, not intended for each symbol to be dissected.
Lake of Fire	A description of Hell or Gehenna which is an eternal fire.
Little Horn	This is the person usually referred to as the Antichrist. He will make war against the saints for three-and-a-half years (Daniel 7:8, 20-27).
Man of Lawlessness	Another name for the person usually referred to as the Antichrist (2 Thessalonians 2:3).

Mark of the Beast	Indication of allegiance to the beast or Antichrist. May literally be a physical indication, but could be related to an Antichrist festival like the feast of Unleavened Bread was a figurative sing on the hand and forehead (Exodus 13:9).
Mid-Tribulation	The Futurist Pre-Millennial view that the rapture will take place three-and-a-half years into the seven-year tribulation.
Mid-Trib	Short for Mid-Tribulation
Millennium	A one thousand year, or long period of Christs rule.
New Jerusalem	Seen with the New Heavens, and New Earth (Revelation 21:1-2). This is the dwelling place Jesus went to prepare for believers (John 14:2) where God will dwell among believers (Revelation 21:3). It is also the bride of Christ (Revelation 21:9-10). It seems to symbolize both a place and a people.
Olivet Discourse	Jesus teachings on the Mount of Olives, a few days before the crucifixion, about the end of the age.

Partial Preterist	View that most of Matthew 24 and Revelation has been fulfilled by 70 AD.
Post-Millennial	Jesus will return after a literal 1,000 year spiritual kingdom, but we do not know when the 1,000 years start.
Post-Tribulation	Pre-Millennial rapture view that the rapture will take place at the end of the seven year tribulation.
Post-Trib	Short for Post-Tribulation
Pre-Millennial	Jesus will return before a literal 1,000-year physical kingdom.
Pre-Tribulation	Pre-Millennial rapture view that the rapture will be before the seven-year tribulation.
Pre-Trib	Short for Pre-Tribulation
Pre-Wrath	Pre-Millennial rapture view that Christ will return before the wrath of God, between the sixth and seventh seals in Revelation.
Preterist	View that all of Matthew 24 and Revelation has been fulfilled by 70 AD.

Prince	Another name for what is commonly called the Antichrist. This term is used in Daniel 9:26-27, sometimes translated ruler.
Rapture	From Latin, for the phrase "caught up" (1 Thessalonians 4:17). A gathering in the sky of living believers.
Rapture Fusion	Rapture view that takes the best of each of the four traditional Pre-Millennial rapture views and merges them into something better. Holds that the rapture will take place after the tribulation (Matthew 24:29-31), between the sixth (Revelation 6:12-17) and seventh seals (Revelation 8:1), at the seventh (Revelation 11:15-17) and last trumpet (1 Corinthians 15:51-52), before the wrath of God (Revelation 6:16-17, 11:18, 16).

Recapitulation	The process of going over a subject again. It is cycling through a time period over and over. Recapitulation, or parallelism, is used to describe how the various sections of Revelation run in parallel to each other. In layman's terms, recapitulation is an instant replay from a different angle.
Resurrection	When the dead are brought to life. One resurrection will immediately precede the rapture of those who are alive (1 Thessalonians 4:16).
Ruler	Another name for what is commonly called the Antichrist. This term is used in Daniel 9:26-27, sometimes translated prince.
Scroll	Sometimes translated book. In Revelation the scroll had seven seals, and was the book of life (Revelation 13:8).
Seal	Literally, a wax seal to protect important documents from being opened by the wrong person. Spiritually, seals of protection that are either broken, or placed.

Second Coming	Jesus Christ's next return to Earth. While the second coming of the Lord is written about throughout the Bible, the enumeration is only mentioned in Hebrews 9:28.
Second Death	The lake of fire, or Hell. For those not found in the book/scroll of life (Revelation 20:14-15). This is contrasted with the second life the resurrected receive.
Seventieth Seven	The last of the seventy seven-year periods mentioned in Daniel 9:24-27. Also known as the seven year tribulation.
Seventieth Week	A translation of the Seventieth Seven, since a week is a unit of seven (Daniel 9:27).
Seven-Year Tribulation	A description of the Seventieth Seven.
Slain Lamb	A metaphor for Jesus. Purchased men with its blood (Revelation 5:6-9). Owner of the Book of Life (Revelation 13:8)
Son of destruction	Another name for the person usually referred to as the Antichrist (2 Thessalonians 2:3).

Star	The stars in Revelation 1:20 were said to symbolize angels or messengers. The star in Revelation 9:1 used a key to open the bottomless pit to free the [fallen] angel of the abyss Apollyon. The stars in Revelation 12:4 are Satan's angels in Revelation 12:9.
Thunders	Found in the throne room of God (Revelation 4:5, Revelation 8:5, and Revelation 11:19), and seven thunders have voices in Revelation 10:3.
Tribulation	Generally any time of trouble. Often used to specifically refer to the seven year tribulation. Is not to be confused with wrath.
Trumpets	Were used to announce what is to come. The rapture and resurrection take place at the last trumpet (1 Corinthians 15:51-52). Jesus receives His kingdom at the last of the seven trumpets in Revelation 11:15-19.

Wormwood	The name of the star which symbolizes a fallen angel who makes a third of the fresh water bitter (Revelation 8:11). The star/demon then uses a key to open the bottomless pit filled with demonic locust including Apollyon (Revelation 9:1-12). The demon Wormwood likely empowers the False Prophet described in Revelation 13:11-18, 16:13-16, and 19:20.
Wrath of God	God's judgment via the seven bowls (Revelation 15-16).

Bible Reference Index

Genesis 6:1-4..158
Genesis 37:9-10...33
Exodus 13:9...213
Leviticus 25...37
Leviticus 25:1-5...31
Deuteronomy 4:32..27
Deuteronomy 13:7..27
Deuteronomy 28:64...27
2 Chronicles 36..37
2 Chronicles 36:20-21..30
Nehemiah 2...31
Psalm 50:10..14
Isaiah 27:12-13..44
Isaiah 27:13...44
Isaiah 61...36, 37
Isaiah 61:1-2..36
Isaiah 61:1-3..35
Isaiah 61:2..36
Isaiah 62:4...186
Jeremiah 25:33...27
Ezekiel 33:2-6...97
Daniel 2...78
Daniel 2:44..78
Daniel 7:8..212
Daniel 7:13-14...79
Daniel 7:20-27..212
Daniel 7:25..47
Daniel 8:5-8..9
Daniel 8:5-8, 21-22...9
Daniel 8:21-22..9
Daniel 9...37

Daniel 9:2...30
Daniel 9:24...36
Daniel 9:24-27...............................28, 29, 31, 34, 217
Daniel 9:25..9, 10, 31
Daniel 9:26..31, 32, 34
Daniel 9:26-27....................................103, 215, 216
Daniel 9:27...28, 34, 36, 39, 41, 42, 47, 52, 62, 72, 73, 134, 135, 167, 168, 169, 173, 174, 207, 217
Daniel 11:31..34, 207
Daniel 11:36-12:13..103
Daniel 12...163
Daniel 12:1...163
Daniel 12:1-4...163
Daniel 12:2...67, 163
Daniel 12:7...47
Daniel 12:11...34, 47
Hosea 2:16..186
Hosea 11:1..77
Joel 2:30-32..109
Joel 2:31..58, 59, 192
Zephaniah 1:7..94, 95
Zephaniah 1:14-16......................................95, 96
Zechariah 2:10-13......................................95, 96
Zechariah 4...106
Zechariah 9:14..44
Zechariah 9:14-16..45
Zechariah 14:4-6...........................192, 193, 200
Malachi 4:5...63, 109
Matthew 2:15..77
Matthew 2:16...112
Matthew 6:10...16, 83
Matthew 21...31
Matthew 22:10..186

Matthew 24....3, 8, 28, 33, 36, 37, 42, 55, 56, 60, 72, 73, 88, 89, 138, 139, 142, 144, 145, 155, 170, 196, 199, 200, 201, 214, 215

Matthew 24:3-31...56

Matthew 24:3-5...56

Matthew 24:4..3

Matthew 24:4-15...145

Matthew 24:6..56

Matthew 24:7..56

Matthew 24:9-28..56

Matthew 24:10-11..3

Matthew 24:15........................34, 53, 60, 89, 169, 199, 207

Matthew 24:15..89

Matthew 24:15-16...33, 36, 113

Matthew 24:15-29..52

Matthew 24:15-31...145

Matthew 24:21...211

Matthew 24:22...159

Matthew 24:24...4, 210, 211

Matthew 24:29...89, 145, 199

Matthew 24:29-3127, 28, 42, 55, 56, 57, 58, 59, 72, 73, 89, 134, 138, 139, 142, 144, 145, 155, 156, 169, 192, 193, 196, 197, 199, 200, 202, 203, 215

Matthew 24:30-31...8

Matthew 24:31...........................43, 53, 54, 60, 89, 197, 201

Matthew 24:34...8

Matthew 25:1...187

Matthew 25:14-30..204

Mark 13...3, 55, 170

Mark 13:4-6...56

Mark 13:7..56

Mark 13:8..56

Mark 13:9-23..56

Mark 13:14..207

Mark 13:24-27...56, 197
Mark 13:27...197
Mark 13:37...197
Luke 1:3..78
Luke 4..37
Luke 4:16-21...35
Luke 15:11-32..64
Luke 17:21...14, 108
Luke 21..3
Luke 21:7-8...56
Luke 21:9-10...56
Luke 21:11...56
Luke 21:12-24..56
Luke 21:20...207
Luke 21:25-28..56
Luke 23:35..197, 210
John 1:14..78
John 3:16...206
John 5..170
John 5:28-29...170, 171, 172
John 14:1-4............38, 39, 43, 49, 55, 60, 155, 165, 167, 170, 173, 182
John 14:2...213
John 17:15...178
Acts 1:11...63
Acts 1:9-11..152
Acts 17:11...5
Acts 28:14-16..64
Romans 2:5...136, 138, 144
Romans 4..37
Romans 4:16...34
Romans 6:23...127, 162
Romans 16:13...197, 210
1 Corinthians 15...170

1 Corinthians 15:22-24..66
1 Corinthians 15:42..49
1 Corinthians 15:51-52....42, 43, 44, 45, 46, 72, 73, 89, 90, 111, 134, 138, 141, 144, 145, 156, 167, 168, 183, 198, 203, 215, 218, 235
1 Corinthians 15:52..156, 201, 202
2 Corinthians 11:2..39, 40, 174, 185
Ephesians 5:31-32..185
Colossians 3:10-12...197, 210
1 Thessalonians 1:10...........................37, 72, 73, 90, 134, 135, 144
1 Thessalonians 4..170
1 Thessalonians 4:15-17...67, 143, 197, 198
1 Thessalonians 4:16...........................28, 41, 52, 62, 63, 93, 202, 216
1 Thessalonians 4:16-17.................................24, 43, 89, 90, 156, 201
1 Thessalonians 4:16..93
1 Thessalonians 4:17........................24, 28, 42, 52, 62, 63, 64, 215
1 Thessalonians 5..185
1 Thessalonians 5:2..184
1 Thessalonians 5:4-6...185
1 Thessalonians 5:9. 37, 39, 43, 48, 63, 67, 72, 73, 90, 135, 144, 151, 160, 167, 170, 173, 174
2 Thessalonians 2...170, 193
2 Thessalonians 2:1..192
2 Thessalonians 2:1-12...191
2 Thessalonians 2:1-3..4
2 Thessalonians 2:1-4...................................42, 47, 48, 103, 167, 169
2 Thessalonians 2:2..192
2 Thessalonians 2:3...193, 205, 212, 217
2 Thessalonians 2:4...194, 202, 207
2 Thessalonians 2:5-12...195
1 Timothy 5:20..197, 210
Hebrews 9:28......................28, 42, 52, 62, 63, 73, 134, 143, 151, 217
1 Peter 3:18-20..158
2 Peter 2:4-5...158

2 Peter 3:8..184
1 John 2:18.....................................103, 115, 208
1 John 2:27-28...82
Jude 1:6-8...158
Revelation 1.....10, 85, 91, 96, 99, 106, 108, 111, 113, 114, 116, 119, 121, 125, 130
Revelation 1-19.............................20, 39, 173, 179
Revelation 1-20...20
Revelation 1-3..............................20, 39, 179, 181
Revelation 1:1-8...85
Revelation 1:3...9
Revelation 1:4.................................108, 156, 181
Revelation 1:7...105
Revelation 1:8...108
Revelation 1:9-20...85
Revelation 1:15-16...105
Revelation 1:18..195
Revelation 1:19..........................10, 11, 86, 177, 182
Revelation 2-3....10, 85, 86, 91, 96, 99, 106, 108, 111, 113, 114, 116, 119, 121, 125, 130
Revelation 2:1-7...85
Revelation 2:8-11...85
Revelation 2:12-17...85
Revelation 2:18-29...85
Revelation 3:1-6...85
Revelation 3:7-13...85
Revelation 3:10...............38, 39, 173, 177, 178, 179
Revelation 3:14-22...85
Revelation 3:16...5
Revelation 3:17...6
Revelation 3:20...6
Revelation 4..87, 99
Revelation 4-19..............20, 26, 37, 38, 39, 173, 179

Revelation 4-22..20, 24, 85, 86, 91, 96, 106, 108, 111, 113, 114, 116, 119, 121, 125, 130, 211
Revelation 4-5..97
Revelation 4-685, 87, 91, 96, 106, 108, 111, 113, 114, 116, 119, 121, 125, 130
Revelation 4:1...37, 38, 39, 173, 182
Revelation 4:1-2...182
Revelation 4:5...218
Revelation 4:8..94, 108
Revelation 5..87, 163, 164
Revelation 5:1-8:1...164
Revelation 5:3...161
Revelation 5:6...112, 161
Revelation 5:6-9..217
Revelation 5:7...161
Revelation 5:8...181
Revelation 5:9...161, 162, 209
Revelation 5:10...17
Revelation 6...52, 87, 88, 99
Revelation 6:1-2..56
Revelation 6:1-8...145
Revelation 6:1-8:1...99
Revelation 6:3-4..56
Revelation 6:5-6..56
Revelation 6:7-8..56
Revelation 6:8..92
Revelation 6:9..93
Revelation 6:9-11...............................56, 138, 140, 144, 145
Revelation 6:11...26, 93
Revelation 6:12. .53, 55, 57, 58, 88, 89, 120, 138, 139, 145, 155, 174, 199, 203, 215
Revelation 6:12-14.......55, 73, 120, 134, 138, 139, 144, 145, 155, 199
Revelation 6:12-17...............53, 56, 57, 58, 88, 89, 153, 199, 203, 215

Revelation 6:14...91, 117, 126, 155

Revelation 6:15-17.....................55, 59, 72, 73, 90, 91, 134, 155, 157

Revelation 6:16..........59, 118, 119, 135, 136, 144, 153, 175, 203, 215

Revelation 6:16-17......................................59, 153, 157, 175, 203, 215

Revelation 6:17..92

Revelation 7...52

Revelation 7-8:1...85, 91, 96, 106, 108, 111, 113, 114, 116, 119, 122, 125, 130

Revelation 7:1...99

Revelation 7:1-3...145

Revelation 7:1-8...91, 96

Revelation 7:1-8:1..96

Revelation 7:3...99

Revelation 7:3-4...92

Revelation 7:9.............................53, 92, 93, 117, 126, 138, 139, 144

Revelation 7:14..211

Revelation 8...93

Revelation 8-11...............................42, 46, 73, 134, 156, 167, 168

Revelation 8:1......93, 94, 118, 119, 135, 136, 144, 145, 195, 203, 215

Revelation 8:2...96, 98, 202

Revelation 8:2-10:11..85, 96, 106, 108, 111, 113, 115, 116, 119, 122, 125, 130

Revelation 8:2-6..97, 98

Revelation 8:2-9:21...99

Revelation 8:3...98

Revelation 8:3-4...181

Revelation 8:4...98

Revelation 8:5...98, 218

Revelation 8:6...98

Revelation 8:7...100, 145

Revelation 8:8...100, 101, 160

Revelation 8:8-9...102

Revelation 8:8-9:12..145

Revelation 8:10-11..102, 160, 195
Revelation 8:11..211, 219
Revelation 8:12..102, 158, 159
Revelation 9:1..................................102, 103, 105, 160, 195, 196
Revelation 9:1-12..219
Revelation 9:1-2..103
Revelation 9:4..54
Revelation 9:5..52, 54, 60, 199
Revelation 9:10..9
Revelation 9:11..103, 158, 196, 208
Revelation 9:12..102
Revelation 9:13-14..104
Revelation 9:13-21..105, 145
Revelation 9:14..158
Revelation 9:16..104
Revelation 10..99, 104
Revelation 10:1..................................105, 123, 145, 204
Revelation 10:1-2..123
Revelation 10:1-3..105
Revelation 10:1-4..145
Revelation 10:2..105
Revelation 10:3..218
Revelation 10:3-4..106, 120
Revelation 10:7..45
Revelation 10:8-11..105
Revelation 10:10-11..204
Revelation 11..104, 107, 111
Revelation 11:1-11:13......85, 106, 108, 111, 113, 115, 116, 119, 122, 125, 130
Revelation 11:1-13..................................99, 106, 108, 111
Revelation 11:2..9, 47
Revelation 11:3..47, 84
Revelation 11:4..106, 107

Revelation 11:7..103, 107, 209

Revelation 11:11-13...107

Revelation 11:12..138, 140, 144

Revelation 11:13..120, 121, 136, 137, 144

Revelation 11:14-11:19....85, 108, 111, 114, 115, 116, 119, 122, 126, 130

Revelation 11:14-19..84, 87, 99, 111

Revelation 11:15. .42, 43, 46, 72, 73, 83, 84, 110, 117, 123, 124, 126, 134, 138, 140, 142, 145, 156, 157, 167, 168, 174, 201, 203, 215

Revelation 11:15-17.42, 43, 72, 73, 83, 123, 134, 138, 140, 142, 144, 145, 167, 168, 203, 215, 235

Revelation 11:15-19..84, 110, 218

Revelation 11:18......59, 109, 118, 119, 136, 137, 144, 153, 157, 158, 175, 181, 203, 215

Revelation 11:18-19..83

Revelation 11:19..106, 107, 218

Revelation 12......................................32, 33, 34, 37, 49, 83, 99, 114

Revelation 12:1-6.84, 85, 87, 112, 113, 114, 115, 117, 119, 122, 126, 130

Revelation 12:4...3, 102, 112, 158

Revelation 12:5...33, 84

Revelation 12:6...47, 84, 112, 179

Revelation 12:7-17..............85, 113, 114, 115, 117, 119, 122, 126, 130

Revelation 12:9...101, 102, 159, 160

Revelation 12:10...102

Revelation 12:10-11...87

Revelation 12:12-14...145

Revelation 12:13...102

Revelation 12:14...33, 36, 47, 50

Revelation 12:14-17..32

Revelation 12:17...33, 50, 114

Revelation 13...99, 117

Revelation 13:1-10...8, 103, 115, 209

Revelation 13:1-14:5.....................85, 115, 117, 119, 122, 126, 130
Revelation 13:4-5..47
Revelation 13:5...47
Revelation 13:5-8..54
Revelation 13:7-10...181
Revelation 13:8..164, 165, 209, 216, 217
Revelation 13:9...81, 161, 165
Revelation 13:11-18..8, 102, 115, 209, 219
Revelation 13:16-18..115
Revelation 14..115, 116, 117
Revelation 14:1........115, 116, 117, 118, 119, 123, 136, 137, 144, 146
Revelation 14:1-5.................................99, 115, 116, 117, 146
Revelation 14:5..117
Revelation 14:6..117
Revelation 14:6-20.............................85, 99, 117, 119, 122, 126, 130
Revelation 14:12...181
Revelation 14:14-16..............................117, 126, 138, 141, 144, 180
Revelation 14:19.....................................118, 119, 136, 137, 144
Revelation 14:20...118, 124
Revelation 15..119
Revelation 15-16..........85, 99, 109, 119, 121, 122, 126, 130, 153, 219
Revelation 15:1-2..141, 144
Revelation 15:1-3...138
Revelation 15:7...153, 162
Revelation 15:7-8..94, 96
Revelation 15:8...136, 144
Revelation 16......................59, 63, 119, 145, 157, 174, 175, 203, 215
Revelation 16:1.........................49, 68, 106, 115, 136, 137, 144, 174
Revelation 16:6..181
Revelation 16:13..211
Revelation 16:13-16...102, 219
Revelation 16:16..120
Revelation 16:18...106, 136, 137, 144

Revelation 16:18-19..136, 137, 144

Revelation 16:18,...107

Revelation 16:20-21..121

Revelation 17...122

Revelation 17:1-20:3..............................86, 122, 126, 130

Revelation 17:6..181

Revelation 17:8..103

Revelation 18:4....................................122, 138, 142, 144

Revelation 18:8...138, 144

Revelation 18:20-24..181

Revelation 19...99, 116, 124

Revelation 19:6..124

Revelation 19:8..181

Revelation 19:11..63, 116

Revelation 19:11-16...9

Revelation 19:11-21...63, 116

Revelation 19:15..119

Revelation 19:16..124

Revelation 19:19-21...124, 125

Revelation 19:20.....................102, 103, 124, 146, 219

Revelation 19:20-21...146

Revelation 19:21..116

Revelation 20.............................20, 99, 109, 172

Revelation 20:1-10...207

Revelation 20:3..124, 125

Revelation 20:4......16, 26, 28, 40, 42, 43, 49, 168, 169, 170, 173, 183

Revelation 20:4-22:21...............................86, 126, 130

Revelation 20:4-5...152

Revelation 20:4-6.....28, 42, 52, 62, 63, 64, 65, 72, 73, 126, 127, 134, 138, 142, 144, 146, 151, 171, 180, 181

Revelation 20:5..164

Revelation 20:6..170

Revelation 20:9..181

Revelation 20:9-10...112
Revelation 20:11-15...28, 42, 52, 62
Revelation 20:12..164, 209
Revelation 20:14...............................28, 65, 102, 127, 143, 171
Revelation 20:14-15...28, 65, 171, 217
Revelation 20:15...............................136, 138, 144, 164, 209
Revelation 21-22..20
Revelation 21:1-2..213
Revelation 21:1-22:5...99
Revelation 21:1-3..166
Revelation 21:3...213
Revelation 21:9-10...187, 213
Revelation 22..181
Revelation 22:6-21...99
Revelation 22:7....................................39, 40, 174, 183, 184
Revelation 22:9...9

About the Author

I have been a Christian as long as I can remember and was baptized at the age of 12. My wife, Elisabeth, and I were married in 2004, and we have three sons. I enjoy playing board games, and am in the process of designing my own. I am employed as a software engineer for a defense contractor. My formal Christian education ended with an 8th grade religion class, but my informal biblical education has persisted since, and has even led to teaching opportunities.

In addition to teaching eschatology (the study of the end times), I am passionate about teaching believers about spiritual gifts, especially from Romans 12. Every believer should know their gift, or be actively trying to identify it, so they can best help the body of Christ function properly. I am inspired by and like to share the testimony of George Müller, a pastor who set out to show his church that God still answers prayer. Müller fed, housed, and educated more than 10,000 orphans, supported more than 100 missionaries (including Hudson Taylor), distributed nearly 2,000,000 Bibles, etc. all through God's provision, as a result of prayer alone.

I became hooked on eschatology during a small group study of the book of Daniel. During this study, I learned about the exact fulfillment of Daniel's prophesy from Daniel 9:25. After calculating the years from Daniel 9:25 and adding them to the start date given in Nehemiah 2, the calculated date for the Messiah is the day of Jesus triumphal entry into Jerusalem, precisely fulfilling the prophesy of Daniel 9:25.

During the same study of Daniel, we discussed the connection between the future resurrection in 1 Corinthians 15:51-52 and the world becoming Christ's kingdom in Revelation 11:15-17. That discussion prompted more than ten years of personal scripture examination and the eventual desire to share what I've learned through writing *Rapture Fusion*.

Come Lord Jesus. Come!

Made in the USA
Monee, IL
14 January 2020